EMPOWERING
THE
CREATIVE
LEADER IN

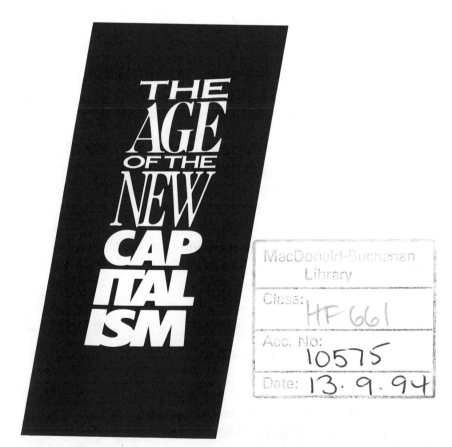

THE
AGE
OF THE
NEW
CAP
ITAL
ISM

Robert R. Carkhuff, Ph.D.

Published by Human Resource Development Press, Inc.
22 Amherst Road
Amherst, Massachusetts 01002

ISBN No. 0-87425-092-7
First Printing, January 1989

Word Processing by Susan Kotzin
Typesetting by The Magazine Group
Illustrations by Image Matrix, Inc.

TO

Carl and Norman Turner,
C.E.O. and Manager, respectively, G.E. Solid State Division,
exemplars in developing human and information capital
as the prepotent sources of economic productivity growth.

FOREWORD

THE DNA OF CREATIVE LEADERSHIP IN THE AGE OF THE NEW CAPITALISM

When most corporate executives are asked to define their mission, they respond, "It is in transition." And it is no wonder. The rapid changes ushered in by the Information Age have created chaos in corporations world-wide. These changes constantly demand new transitions.

In his most recent books, *The Age of the New Capitalism,* and *The Creative Leader in the Age of the New Capitalism,* Robert Carkhuff provides a perspective and framework that will enable executives to obtain a new sense of order and direction as they prepare for the twenty-first century.

Carkhuff begins by giving us a vision of the old, financial-capital-based capitalisms—a weak capitalism that, through corporate machinations, is being drained of its last vestiges of potency. Defining capital as "most important," Carkhuff counters with a vision of the new, human- and information- capital-based capitalism—a robust capitalism that promises accelerating productivity and profitability for consumer as well as producer. Carkhuff is telling us that it is not our implementation of the old capitalism that is wrong; it is the system itself that has outlived its usefulness. In short, for Carkhuff, capitalism is, itself, a theory of change, and he delivers to us a path-finding vision of its future.

This foreword will compare current corporate norms with Carkhuff's vision of what is possible in regard to:
- Mission
- Strategies
- Performance indicators and
- Education and training

This vision provides the images and systems that will guide Corporate America back into world leadership in the next century. You will see, deductively and systematically, how organizations and individuals can be empowered to take charge. And you will see how the core educational skills of thinking, relating, and planning break the genetic code of culture change.

DEFINING THE CORPORATE MISSION

The Current Corporate Norm

Most organizations define their mission in terms of corporate productivity and profitability. Rarely do organizations establish a mission that includes consumer benefits. In the twenty-first century, consumers will make purchasing decisions based on the degree to which a vendor is able to satisfy their productivity and profitability goals. And their ability to purchase will be directly related to their ability to achieve those goals. Currently, corporations are not thinking systematically about how they can help their customers improve every phase of their business.

The Carkhuff Vision

The Carkhuff vision provides a framework that enables executives to translate data and values into a mission and strategies. It facilitates the exploration of questions such as, "How can our products and services help our customers improve their marketing, distribution, production, and resource functions?" It encourages executives to reflect upon their values and create strategies that benefit their organization and their clients' organizations.

DEVELOPING CORPORATE STRATEGIES

The Current Corporate Norm

Most organizations develop their strategies in the areas of marketing, distribution, production, and finance. Usually, most decisions are made predominantly on the basis of short-term financial considerations. Unfortunately for most American corporations, in the Age of Information, 85 percent of economic productivity growth is due to the synergistic interaction of human capital (HC) and information capital (IC). HC is the source of the next, market-sensitive idea. IC is the operational system for the last idea. While HC and IC will clearly create the future, the sad fact is that these sources of variance for high performance are either entirely absent or receive token attention in corporate strategy formulation.

The Carkhuff Vision

The Carkhuff vision provides a framework for management to translate the mission and strategies developed by executives into goals and systems at all levels. Most important, the strategy for the resource component includes plans not only for ensuring that financial resources are optimally invested to serve as a catalyst for short-term growth, but also for transforming human and information resources into HC and IC to serve as catalysts for long-term growth. As such, human- and information-resource development becomes an integrated and vital part of business strategy.

CREATING PERFORMANCE INDICATORS

The Current Corporate Norm

Most organizations have multitudinal performance appraisals that are conducted infrequently and perceived resentfully. It is rare when corporations recognize an individual's contribution to the team or the team's contribution to the organization. Most typically, organizations suffer from turfism and provincialism. In these organizations more energy is directed inward to protect self-interest than outward to enhance consumer growth.

The Carkhuff Vision

The Carkhuff vision provides a framework for supervisors to translate goals and systems into specific objectives and programs. The emphasis is upon teamwork and "frontline processing." The individual is encouraged to think independently and relate interdependently with other team members, and the unit is rewarded for working interdependently with other departments within the organization and with client organizations. Employees are rewarded not only for meeting individual objectives, but also for contributions they make to their team, their organization, and their customers.

EDUCATION AND TRAINING

The Current Corporate Norm

Most organizations offer a smorgasbord of training programs in a variety of functional, specialty skills. The quality and quantity of these programs vary, but the common theme is to take a fragmented approach. The content orientation is typically on facts and concepts. The teaching methodology primarily consists of didactic presentations and examples of "excellent performance" which review and overview critical functions and skills. There is usually minimal emphasis on skills mastery and application, and learners leave training with insufficient understanding to transfer learnings to their jobs.

The Carkhuff Vision

The Carkhuff vision provides a framework that can serve as the educational core. Learners master the skills of thinking, relating, and planning that they can use immediately to develop objectives and programs within each of the systems described above at their level of intervention. The organization supports their use of those skills through periodic training supplements in the functional areas. As a result of education in the core curriculum and training in the functional areas, employees become empowered to create systems of their own in which objectives and plans are developed. Employees not only develop the capacity to think independently, they learn how to relate their ideas in a constructive and systematic fashion. Information flows up and down in the organizations. Ideas are shared vertically and horizontally. Thinking relationships are formed with internal and external clients. Constructive, "capital-based," corporate culture change is no longer leader dependent; and leaders are not naive enough to depend upon "one-minute" treatments.

CHANGING THE CORPORATE CULTURE

The Current Corporate Norm

The norm in organizations today is to maximize efficiency by downsizing, restructuring, and other machinations. This sometimes maximizes short-term profit. The problem is that it also minimizes long-term economic growth. By emphasizing the efficiency of financial capital investments, the corporation suffers the loss of invaluable human and information capital. Simply stated, the talent leaves and takes with it invaluable information capital gained from different projects. Ultimately, the issue is one of trust between the employee and the corporation. The employee asks, "Will the corporation look out for me after I think myself out of my job?" In turn, the corporation asks, "Will the employees invest themselves in the corporations which taught them to think?"

The Carkhuff Vision

The Carkhuff vision has three cornerstones: 1) the business operations, which become a thinking center; 2) the educational operations, which become a thinking skills center; 3) the marketing operations, which become a thinking market. The educational center is the source of productive thinking skills. The personnel are empowered to implement a productive thinking environment. In turn, the thinking environment empowers the consumers by educating them in a thinking marketing relationship. Together, these sources constitute the cornerstones of the New Capitalism.

To sum, Carkhuff's visionary work has contributed the DNA of creative leadership in the Age of the New Capitalism. In so doing, Carkhuff puts the choice squarely before us: to continue the old, financial- capital-based capitalism which yields diminishing returns and accelerating investments, or to commit to the new, human- and information- capital-based capitalism which yields potentially infinite returns and infinitesimal investments beyond thinking people and the operational information they produce. In short, the choice is between the life or death of capitalism—and with it the freedom or totalitarianism of humankind.

Rick Bellingham, Ph.D.
Vice President, Northern Telecom

ROBERT R. CARKHUFF, PH.D.

- One of the most-cited social scientists of our time and author of three of the most-referenced books over the last two decades.

- Chairman and C.E.O. of Human Technology, Inc., one of the fastest-growing corporations in the U.S.A.

- A visionary of the New Capitalism based upon the new capital ingredients—human and information capital.

PREFACE

The message of this book is simple and straightforward: Empowering is the source of creative leadership in the Age of Information. Empowering involves sharing power and authorizing people to think and make decisions. Moreover, empowering emphasizes skilling people in the thinking skills needed to discharge their responsibilities.

Empowering in the Age of Information emphasizes processing information. We empower organizations when we develop them to maximize information processing. We empower people when we develop their thinking skills.

There are several primary sources for these conclusions:

- The data of economists which indicate that *human and information capital are the critical sources of economic productivity growth in the Age of Information.*
- The research of executives of the fastest-growing corporations indicate that *human processing or productive thinking is the prepotent ingredient in economic productivity growth.*
- My own personal experience at the helm of one of the fastest-growing corporations, indicates that *empowering individuals to think is the single most significant source of economic growth in the Age of Information.*

In the pages that follow, I will attempt to draw upon all of these sources in presenting ten strategies of creative leadership and their relationship to economic growth in the Age of Information—in short, our future!

McLean, Virginia   R.R.C.
October, 1988

ACKNOWLEDGMENTS

First, I am in debt to people—themselves creative leaders—who were in my feedback network in developing these materials:

- Rick Bellingham, Northern Telecom
- Bill Beuhler, AT&T
- Dave Burleigh, Dave Burleigh Associates
- Don Carlson, General Dynamics
- Ed Feder, Tenneco Oil
- Todd Holder, E-Systems
- Jack Kelly and Jack Reilly, IBM
- Carl Turner and Norman Turner, General Electric

Second, in preparing these materials, I owe my gratitude to the following people who are a creative part of most of the things that I do:

- Bernard Berenson, American International College
- John Cannon, Alex Douds, Sharon Fisher, Richard Pierce, Ray Vitalo and Don Benoit, Human Technology, Inc.
- Cheryl Aspy and Dave Aspy, Carkhuff Institute of Human Technology
- Jim Barnet, Northern Alberta Institute of Technology
- Ken Levy, Johnson and Wales College

Finally, I owe a special debt of gratitude to the people who have helped me to publish and market the material:

- My wife, Bernice, who has done this many times over.
- Susan Kotzin who has endured the typing iterations.
- My son, Bob, who facilitated the publishing and marketing.

R.R.C.

TABLE OF CONTENTS

I. INTRODUCTION AND OVERVIEW—
THE CREATIVE LEADER AND EMPOWERING FOR GROWTH

Empowering is the theme of the creative leader. This leader recognizes that we are entering the Age of the New Capitalism. The new capital ingredients emphasize the ideas of human capital and the operations of information capital. The creative leader capitalizes fully by investing in human- and information-capital development and, then, freeing these ingredients to operate in the workplace and the marketplace. The New Capitalism is defined by these vital sources of economic productivity growth. The mission that thinking leaders define and the strategic plans they develop are the most highly leveraged sources of economic growth in the Age of the New Capitalism.

THE CREATIVE LEADER

We may illustrate empowering organizations with a case study. National Cash Register Co. (NCR) was knocked out of a dominant position in the marketplace in the early 1970s by a wave of electronic cash registers and adding machines. "No doubt about it. We didn't react quickly enough," said Elton White, NCR executive vice president for product marketing and strategic planning. "We didn't pay enough attention to trends." This is where the problem began for NCR. The leaders of NCR managed to turn market share and earnings around by implementing principles of creative organizations. First, NCR paid attention to trends. Indeed, it guided its future organization by market information. Second, NCR reorganized its operations to maximize processing, marketing, and other relevant information. At the same time that it defined its mission to include lines of computer products, it began breaking up an unwieldy monolithic corporation. Simultaneously while it centralized by mission, it decentralized its operations. Similarly, NCR modified its operations to maximize information processing, handing authority for research and product development to more nimble, smaller, independent divisions. Finally, NCR continues to fine-tune all of the operations, emphasizing the human processing that evolves from empowering personnel with both responsibility and authority for processing.

EMPOWERING ORGANIZATIONS

The principles which guided NCR are the characteristics of thinking organizations in the Age of the New Capitalism.

- *They are guided by marketing information which empowers their consumers!*
- *They are centralized by a mission which empowers the organization!*
- *They are decentralized by operations which empowers the operators!*
- *They are modified by operations which empowers the delivery personnel!*
- *They emphasize human processing which empowers all personnel!*

Following these principles enabled NCR to bounce back in the marketplace. The same principles apply to empowering all organizations in meeting the challenges of rapid information change in the Age of the New Capitalism.

THE THINKING ORGANIZATION

We may also illustrate empowering individuals with a case study. Ed Mahler was assigned to the corporate planning staff at DuPont. At about the same time, he decided that artificial intelligence, or AI, was a promising technology that the firm was not using. Without assignment or portfolio, he initiated his AI mission. His thinking culminated in experimenting with personal computer programs that mimicked human experts for specific tasks. He worked together with Dave Penzak, a computer specialist from central research staff, and they designed a strategy for piloting AI programs. They developed processing programs to discharge various organizational functions. They initiated to install pilot programs in nine application areas. They studied the productivity feedback from these programs and concluded that seven of the pilots were successful. Mahler was a creative employee. He exemplified the principles of creative functioning in the organizational context. First, he thought about the goals and problems systematically. Second, he joined forces with Penzak in thinking about the issues interpersonally. Third, with others, he focused upon organizational processing to discharge organizational functions. Fourth, he initiated to experiment responsibly. Fifth, he held himself accountable by recycling productivity feedback.

EMPOWERING INDIVIDUALS

Together, these ingredients defined empowering thinking people in the organizational context:

- Empowering by *thinking better* or thinking systematically!
- Empowering by *relating fully* or processing interpersonally!
- Empowering by *working smarter* or processing organizationally!
- Empowering by *freeing initiative* or initiating responsibly!
- Empowering by *recycling productivity feedback* or being accountable!

These are the principles for empowering individual creativity in the organizational context. For Mahler, these principles led to the "compelling economic returns" of his applications. They also led to organizational promotions. Today, Mahler is DuPont's manager of artificial intelligence, overseeing the application of about five hundred expert systems.

"We have broken so many of the traditional DuPont rules. Five years ago, I would have been fired. Today, I get bonuses."

THINKING PERSONNEL

Historically, during the Industrial Age, financial capital was viewed as the dominant economic ingredient. Financial capital enabled the purchase of land and resources, machinery and labor necessary for production. Indeed, the term capital—meaning "most important"—was seen as synonymous with finances. To be sure, humans were seen as mere extensions of this production machinery. Today, humans and the information they produce are the "most important" sources of economic growth. Human and information capital now account for 85 percent of economic productivity growth, leaving financial capital to serve as a catalytic agent. The prepotency of human and information capital serves to introduce "The Age of the New Capitalism."

Economic Growth

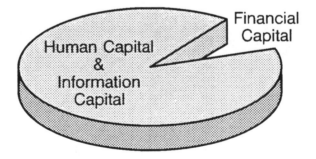

THE AGE OF THE NEW CAPITALISM

The prepotency of human and information capital is accentuated by the economic context. As we transition from the Old Capitalism to the New Capitalism, we are also moving from an economy of scarcity to an economy of abundance. The economy of abundance means that executives no longer have the luxury of a period of time in which demand for innovative products and services will exceed the supply of those products and services. This is because of intensifying technological innovation, dissemination, and initiation. The executive must confront the realities of an economy with a surplus of increasingly cost-beneficial products and services. Those corporations that survive and grow will do so because the leaders understand human and information capital as the source of that growth.

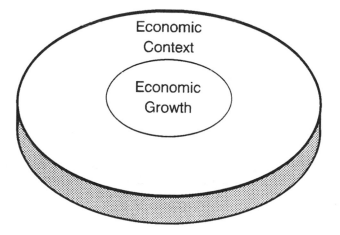

AN ECONOMY OF ABUNDANCE

Who, then, is the creative leader in the Age of the New Capitalism? In order to answer this question, we surveyed a number of sources, including the chief executive officers of the fastest-growing businesses in America. We found that potentially at least, *the creative leader is everyone.* Everyone who heads a unit or supervises a center or managers a division is "in business" and must demonstrate creative leadership and productive outcomes. In this context, chief executives of the growth firms believe the "thinking manager" is their most important asset. Indeed, many of the executives believe that true changes in corporate culture will occur "only when everyone becomes his or her own boss." These chief executives themselves are perhaps the most valuable source of our learning about creative leadership. In the pages that follow, I will attempt to illustrate the operational principles of creative leadership by which they and others are guided.

WHO IS THE CREATIVE LEADER?

Whether their corporations are large or small, creative leaders realize that 90% of the people in the year 2000 will work for firms employing fewer than 200 people. In this context, creative leaders see their primary functions as *taking both entrepreneurial and intrapreneurial initiatives.* Entrepreneurial initiatives involve creating new businesses. Intrapreneurial initiatives emphasize making the old businesses more productive and profitable. In the entrepreneurial context, these leaders see their responsibilities as anticipating, then initiating in the intermediate term, a three-to-five-year future marketplace. In the intrapreneurial context, the leaders see their responsibilities as making immediate decisions concerning the development of the organization and its personnel.

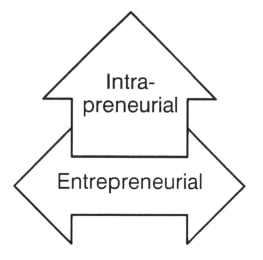

WHAT DOES THE CREATIVE LEADER DO?

If everyone is potentially a leader, then creative leadership takes place *everywhere and all of the time.* Our "information load" is doubling every few years so that we will experience 32 times more "information pressure" in the year 2000 than we do now. Since the information environment is incessant, the human processor has no vacation. The creative leader is continuously immersed in and constantly processing information. Think of the leader as the center of a universe of information that is incessantly changing and growing. The information knows no limits in space or time. The creative leader knows no limits in searching and thinking.

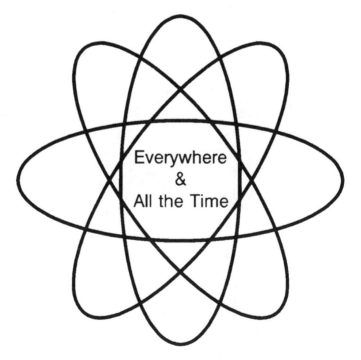

WHERE AND WHEN DOES THE CREATIVE LEADER DO IT?

The big question is, "How does the creative leader discharge the entrepreneurial and intrapreneurial functions?" The answer to this question is "by empowering." Empowering is an act of investing or authorizing, whereby people and organizations are enabled to achieve goals. There are two primary processes in which the creative leader engages to empower others: *organizational and individual.* The first process emphasizes empowering creative organizations to accomplish their mission. The second process emphasizes empowering creative personnel to perform the tasks that accomplish the mission. The empowering of creative organizations is calculated to maximize information processing. The empowering of creative personnel is calculated to maximize the individual processing of information.

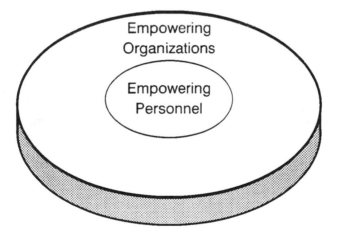

HOW DOES THE CREATIVE LEADER DO IT?

The question "Why?" is the explanation for leadership. Why is the creative leader constantly empowering individuals and organizations to accomplish entrepreneurial and intrapreneurial initiatives? The answer to this question lies in *the motives of the individual and the mission of the organization.* The creative leader is a person whose motives are elevated beyond personal incentives, beyond achievements and, yes, even beyond self-actualization. The truly creative leader is committed to a mission outside of himself or herself. When that individual mission converges with the organizational mission, then all daily tasks have meaning, and both the individual and the organization have a raison d'etre.

WHY DOES THE CREATIVE LEADER DO IT?

There are two primary indices of how well the creative leaders perform: *economic growth and employment growth.* Both economic growth and employment growth reflect innovation in the marketplace. In one sample of economic growth, for example, the surveyed executives head firms that averaged nearly 90 percent yearly growth, ranging over 1,000 percent over a four-year period. In terms of employment growth, their firms averaged 50 percent yearly growth, totaling over 500 percent over a four-year period. By contrast, during the same period, Fortune 500 firms averaged 4 percent yearly economic growth and 3 percent yearly employment loss over the same four-year period. Surely, these creative leaders have something to teach us. In the pages that follow, we will search the principles that guide creative leaders in the Age of the New Capitalism.

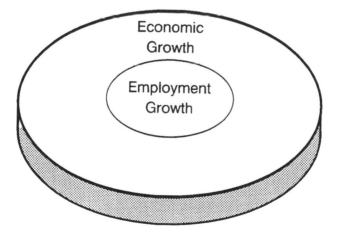

HOW WELL DOES THE CREATIVE LEADER DO?

To sum, the creative leader emphasizes empowering as the source of growth in an economy of abundance. The creative leader views human capital as the source of the next creative idea with which to enter the marketplace. The creative leader views information capital as the operations of the last idea that translate into products and services. Building upon these sources of growth, the creative leader empowers both people and organizations in the workplace and in the marketplace. The creative leader empowers people and organizations by skilling them individually and then relating them interdependently.

Empowering Positioning
for
Growth

POSITIONING FOR GROWTH

II. TEN STRATEGIES TO GUIDE ECONOMIC GROWTH

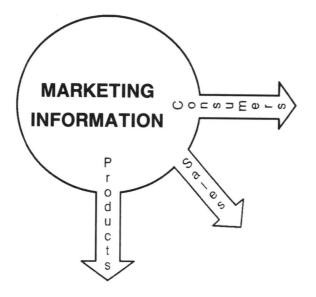

1. Guide by Marketing Information!

"Pogo, the cartoon character, pointed out one time that the way to become a great leader is to see a parade and run like hell to get in front of it. . . . I don't know of many innovations where somebody sort of just dreamed up an idea out of the clear blue and went off. I mean, there are usually some fairly discernible trends available for a long time indicating a demand for a product or a service. And the time to act on that— to get to the front of the parade, if you will—is when the demand, and the technology needed to meet it, begin to converge." (Smith, 1986)

The speaker is Fred Smith, the employer of nearly forty thousand people who once met a payroll by winning at blackjack. Fred is the person who created the overnight delivery at Federal Express. Still viewed as a gambler, Fred sees marketers as "reasonable adventurers," people attuned to consumers who take risks to accomplish things rather than for the thrill of the risks per se.

FINDING A PARADE

*Smith views innovation as a discipline that lends itself to study and practice. As with many successful business people in rapidly changing industries, Smith thinks of innovation not only in terms of opportunity, but increasingly in terms of necessity and survival. Smith uses **U.S.A. Today** to illustrate his point. Whereas television made us a national society, it was not until the technology was developed to send copy via satellite that a national newspaper was made possible. Smith points out that Gannett's Al Neuharth recognized the relegation of the local newspaper by television to local news, and so took advantage of the convergence of societal change and a technology to fulfill the expectation.*

> *"It's at that point that the innovator says to himself, 'Now's the time I ought to take a risk. I see the threat on the supply side. I see the opportunity on the demand side. And, oh, by the way, I'd like to do something new and useful and important.' And when all of that happens, that's when organizations tend to innovate."*

Whereas consumer information tells Smith where the parade is, product information enabled him to get in front of the parade.

TO THE FRONT OF THE PARADE

Smith is also attuned to sales information. Sales information enables him to refine the consumer targets within the parade. Sales information also allows him to fine-tune the products that put him in front of the parade. Yet even Smith sometimes gets too far in front of the parade. Staying finely tuned to sales information, Smith recently gave up—at least temporarily—on Zap Mail service, a product innovation that lost more than $130 million. Smith is a wise executive who knows that escalating commitment to a project independent of sales information is a critical executive mistake.

STAYING IN FRONT OF THE PARADE

24

"Guide by marketing information!" is the first strategy of economic growth. Marketing information is the product of our ongoing sharing of information with our consumers. Marketing information takes three critical forms. Consumer information helps define the target populations. It tells us which parade we wish to join. Product information helps define product innovation. It tells us how to get to the head of the parade. Sales information helps refine both target populations and product innovation. It tells us how to stay at the head of the parade.

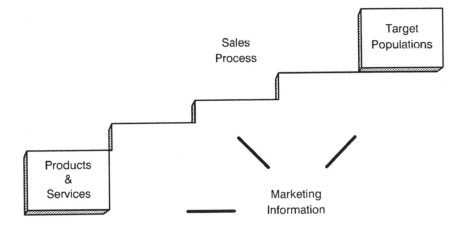

MARKETING INFORMATION

Thus, marketing information contributes to the marketing process. Consumer information enables us to target and segment consumer populations. Product information enables us to innovate and differentiate our product uniqueness in the marketplace. Sales information allows us to interact with consumers to sell our products and services, and with producers, to further innovate the products and services.

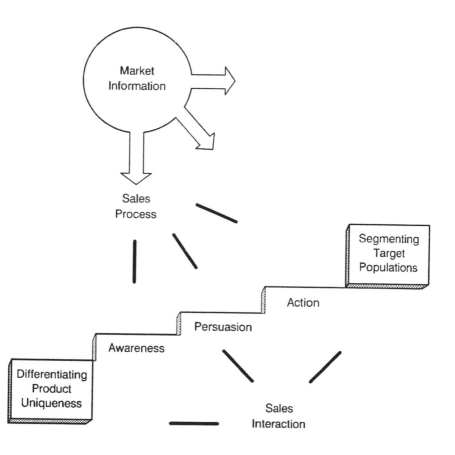

MARKETING INFORMATION ⟶ MARKETING PROCESS

Perhaps the most critical element of marketing is the relationship between producer and consumer. In fact, the creative marketing relationship is balanced, with both consumer and producer receiving information from the other. Indeed, producers and consumers are linked interdependently by the concept of productivity. For producers and consumers alike, productivity is the comparison of costs and benefits that yields profitability. Producer and consumer are inextricably bound: each grows as the other grows. For the producer, this means that those who make their consumers productive will become productive themselves. Put another way, *our business is to keep our consumers in business!*

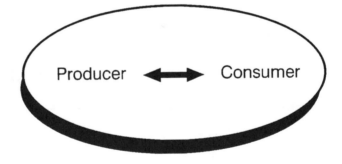

THE MARKETING RELATIONSHIP

The concept of consumer productivity is a new one and a critical one. It is not consumerism! It is not consumer satisfaction! It is not even consumer benefits per se! Rather, it is a comparison of costs and benefits: "Did I get the most of what I value by investing the least of what I value?" Consumer productivity is the guiding ethic of marketing in the Age of Information. And it is indeed an ethic, because those producers who deliver the highest quality products and services for the cheapest prices will in turn derive the most benefits themselves. In this context, the basic information emphasizes not consumer buying habits but, rather, consumer using habits. In other words, the basic information involves areas in which consumers wish to become productive, i.e., maximizing their benefits while minimizing their costs.

Consumer Productivity

CONSUMER INFORMATION

The net effect of the consumer productivity ethic is to empower the consumer. No longer is the consumer a dependent variable in the marketing equation. The consumer is an equal partner in the marketing operations that drive the organization. Producer and consumer relate interdependently, for they are indeed interdependently related. The consumers are empowered by the simple act of ascribing potency to the information they provide. Put another way, in order to accomplish producer goals, the producer must enable the consumer to accomplish consumer goals. In order to be empowered by the information and purchases of the consumer, the producer must first be oriented to empowering the consumer.

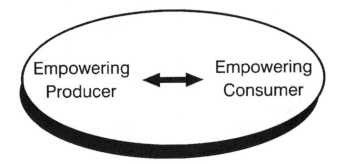

EMPOWERING THE CONSUMER

The meaning for executives is clear. It is the executive's job to establish policy to empower the consumer in the marketing relationship. In this context, it may be helpful to conceive of the marketing relationship as a two-way escalator: producer products and information are put in the hands of the consumers ("going up"); consumer needs and ideas are made available to the producers ("going down"). The vehicle for accomplishing producer benefits in the Age of Information is to empower the consumer to achieve consumer benefits.

EXECUTIVE MEANING OF EMPOWERING BY MARKETING INFORMATION

To sum, we may define marketing in the Information Age as follows:

> Marketing is an interdependent process by which both producers and consumers are empowered to accomplish benefits.

Such a definition leads directly to the mission of the organization. It defines the target populations. It defines products and services directly, and productivity and profitability goals indirectly. It generates the marketing strategies that drive the remaining organizational components—resources, production, distribution. In short, marketing information based upon empowering consumers defines the organizational mission in the Age of Information.

MARKETING INFORMATION ⟶ ORGANIZATION MISSION

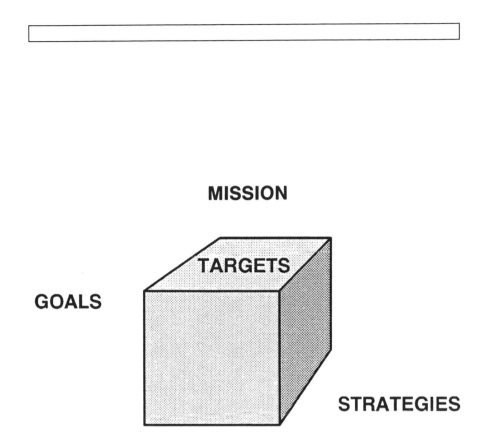

MISSION

TARGETS

GOALS

STRATEGIES

2. Centralize by Mission!

*Ken Hendricks calls the **ABC** corporation "the biggest small company in America." **ABC** stands for American Builders and Contractors Supply Company. **ABC** has risen from a small-town roofing business to become a sixty-two outlet, $183-million-a-year chain of wholesale roofing and siding supply distributorships. Hendricks picked up some of these distributorships as failing independents and others from major manufacturers who were unable to stay solvent in a generally low-margin, high-service industry. **ABC**'s growth curve has been impressive, moving from #3 to #2 to #1 on successive **INC.** 500 lists of the country's fastest-growing corporations (Kahn, 1986).*

THE BIGGEST SMALL COMPANY

According to Hendricks, "What I really am is a renovator." Looking upon the industry with a renovator's eye, Hendricks asked the following "What if..." questions:

- *"What if you combined the product knowledge and customer service of the independents with the financial clout of national chains?*
- *"What if you concentrated on small contractors rather than the big accounts that are more vulnerable to housing-market downturns?*
- *"What if you managed the company in a way designed to exploit the peculiar characteristics of the market?"*

"WHAT IF..."

In answering these questions, Hendricks decided to centralize the support mission and decentralize the distribution operations. In centralizing the support mission, Hendricks centered every facet of the support system—truck leasing, real estate, advertising, even sign painting—in central headquarters. Recognizing cost control as the critical function in a low-margin business, he put all operations under tight budgetary constraints. Thus, a $7,000 storefront sign is put up for $350—overnight. If an **ABC** *truck blows an engine, it is shipped to central headquarters and a new one is forwarded. For these multifaceted services, Hendricks charges the distributors a minimal fee—one percent of gross sales.*

CENTRALIZING THE MISSION

The distributors, in turn, are delegated both responsibility and authority for all local decisions having to do with service to the customer. In addition, they are proffered cash incentives to improve profit margins. Still, if there is a clear message in Hendricks' business practices, it is centralizing by mission. He exerts tight control over every aspect of support services provided to the sixty-two **ABC** *distributorships. When he asserts that he could turn a profit on any hardware store item, he means precisely this: the margins in the wholesale business are primarily in overhead and cost control—in effect in the dozens of tiny details that Hendricks is so good at. For Hendricks, centralizing the mission is as simple as* **ABC**.

AS SIMPLE AS *ABC*

"Centralize by mission!" is the second strategy for economic growth. The goals of the mission are derived from marketing information, specifically the product information that has led to the innovative and differentiated product and services we hope to market. Usually, the goals center around the benefits that will accrue as a consequence of the organization's activities. These benefits emphasize the organization's or producer's benefits. However, as we have seen, the benefits must also include consumer benefits. In the Age of Information, those organizations survive and grow that enable their consumers to survive and grow.

GOALS

- Producer
  Benefits

- Consumer
  Benefits

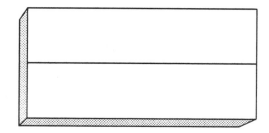

DRIVING BY MARKETING GOALS

The primary targets of the mission are also derived from marketing information, specifically the consumer information that led to targeting and segmenting consumers. The targets emphasize the consumer populations whose needs are being addressed in order to accomplish the consumer and producer benefit goals. The target populations include the internal producer or employee populations that enable the achievement of the goals. In other words, the target populations defined by the mission incorporate people affecting the goals as well as those affected by the goals.

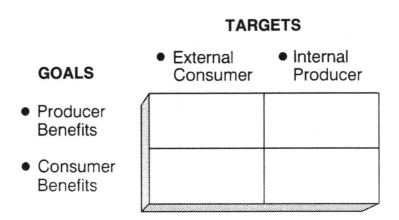

TARGETING SEGMENTED POPULATIONS

Finally, the strategies for accomplishing the goals with the targets are also derived from marketing information, specifically the ongoing sales information that enables us to modify our goals, targets and strategies continuously. In productive organizations, the long-term goals and targets are addressed by continuously changing strategies. The strategies are driven by marketing information; they include marketing, distribution, production, and resource strategies.

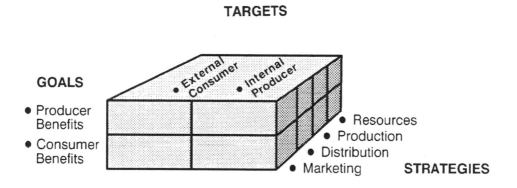

OPERATIONALIZING BY STRATEGIZING

It is only when the mission is defined comprehensively that the organization is empowered. A comprehensive definition includes consumer benefits as well as producer benefits, and producer targets along with consumer targets. Traditionally, organizational missions are defined in terms of one cell— manipulating consumer targets to provide producer benefits, namely profitability. Succinctly stated, ''You can't get there from here!'' Only when the mission is defined to emphasize achieving both productivity and profitability benefits for both producer and consumer is the organization empowered. Indeed, the relationship between mission and organization is a dynamic and interactive one: each is empowered as the other is empowered.

TARGETS

GOALS	• Consumers	• Producers
• Consumer Benefits	Consumer Profitability	Consumer Productivity
• Producer Benefits	Producer Profitability	Producer Productivity

EMPOWERING THE ORGANIZATION

Empowering the organization by defining and centralizing the mission is the raison d'etre for the existence of the organization. Indeed, from an organizational perspective, the mission is the organization: the growth of each is reflected in the growth of the other. In turn, from an organizational perspective, the executive is the living representative of the mission. In short, the mission gives the organization the meaning the executive intended. Like Ken Hendricks' mission, it focuses all operations and gives meaning to the performance of all personnel.

EXECUTIVE MEANING OF EMPOWERING BY CENTRALIZING THE MISSION

42

To sum, we may define the mission in the Information Age as follows:

> The mission is a comprehensive definition of consumer and producer benefits that empowers the organization and guides its operations.

Centralizing the mission focuses the energies, motivation, and intellect of personnel upon productivity and profitability goals for both consumer and producer. Actualizing these goals is the source of the operations centered upon the mission.

CENTRALIZED MISSION ⟶ DECENTRALIZED OPERATIONS

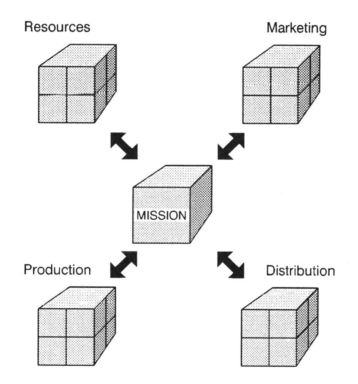

Resources

Marketing

MISSION

Production

Distribution

3. Decentralize by Operations!

A $27 million F-15 is a potent instrument; but without spare parts and skilled mechanics, it soon becomes a useless hunk of metal. That is what General Bill Creech found when he took command of the Tactical Air Command (TAC) in 1978. For all intents and purposes, the procedures for getting a fighter fixed might have been devised by a British labor union steward. At any one time, half of the planes in the $25-billion fleet were not battle ready and more than 220 airplanes were classified as "hangar queens"—grounded at least three weeks for lack of spare parts or maintenance. Because of the equipment problems, TAC pilots—trained at a cost of $1 million each—lacked the flying time necessary to keep their skills sharp. The best of them, along with mechanics and technicians, were quitting the Air Force in droves. Perhaps worst of all was the soaring accident rate that resulted in tragic deaths and loss of equipment.

FLYING LOW

46

Into the breach stepped General Creech. The main problem he saw was centralization installed by McNamara's "whiz kids," for reasons more political than operational. In a highly matrixed system, the functional specialists only loosely worked for the manager. McNamara was a disciple of the management gurus of his day. He preached that centralization was synonymous with efficiency. While the whiz kids devised new military strategies, legions of cost analysts and systems planners cranked out new rules and regulations that governed every facet of military life. Field commanders were stripped of their authority.

"TOP-DOWN" MANAGEMENT

The way General Creech saw it, saving money over-shadowed doing the job. The job was the mission: flying and fighting. Creech made sure that the lowest-level employees understood this centralized mission. In this context, the first thing Creech did was to decentralize his command in smaller and more manageable units—the squadron rather than the larger wing unit. In addition, he created squadron repair teams. His idea was to give the operational squadrons and their companion maintenance teams common identities and common information necessary to their objectives. In short, Creech was able to implement his programs with no more money, no more planes, and no more personnel than his predecessors. His strategy was to force a "bottoms-up" delivery style on an organization that had always been "top-down." He pushed responsibility and authority down to the lowest chain of command.

"BOTTOMS-UP" DELIVERIES

*By the time General Creech left **TAC**, 85 percent of the airplanes were "mission capable." **TAC** was capable of launching six thousand sorties a day, double what it had been when he arrived at Langley. The crash rate was reduced from one for thirteen thousand flying hours to one for fifty thousand; crashes traced to faulty maintenance disappeared. **TAC** went from the Air Force's worst command to its best command. Re-enlistment rates increased dramatically. And only 3 percent of the wing commanders who served under Creech were relieved for poor performance!*

FLYING HIGH

Creech summarized his "Four-Star" Management program as follows:

1. *Workers are more professional when provided with a professional environment.*
2. *Workers take more responsibility when they have a sense of ownership.*
3. *Management control is established through motivation, not regulation.*
4. *Consolidation and centralization can lower output as well as costs.*

Creech concluded:

"It's not really hard to run a large organization. You just have to think small about how to achieve your goals. There's a very finite limit to how much leadership you can exercise at the very top. You can't micromanage—people resent that. Things are achieved by individuals, by collections of twos and fives and twenties, not collections of 115,000. And that's as true in industry as it is in the military." (Finegan, 1987)

FOUR-STAR MANAGEMENT

"Decentralize by operations!" is the third strategy for economic growth. The first task in decentralizing is to clarify the functions of the strategies. In the illustration below, the strategies emphasize the following: selling the consumer; servicing the consumer; making the product; supporting the other functions. While these functions are highly interactive, we may see them moving in a linear manner as indicated below.

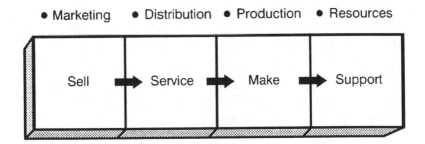

CLARIFYING THE FUNCTIONS

The second task in decentralizing operations is to design the strategic system. We must design the strategic operations before we can decentralize them. In the illustration below, the components of the strategic system are derived directly from the strategies of the mission. The strategic functions are broken down at management, supervision, and delivery levels. The strategic processes include those of the basic processing system: inputs, processing, outputs, feedback.

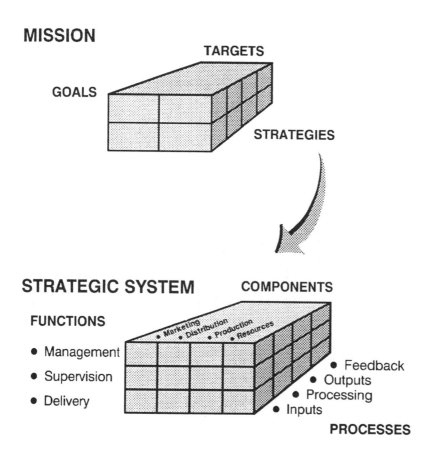

DESIGNING STRATEGIC SYSTEMS

The third task, then, is to decentralize operations. The guiding principle is to maximize information processing. In other words, when the operation has differentiated information needs, it may be decentralized. On the other hand, when operations have similar information needs, they may be clustered. In the illustration below, the operations are decentralized by the components of the strategic design.

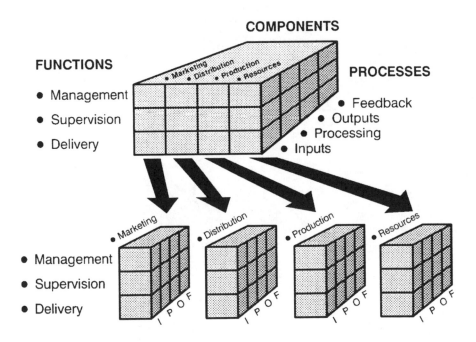

DECENTRALIZING BY INFORMATION NEEDS

Empowering the operations by decentralizing operations is analogous to empowering the organization by centralizing the mission. Just as executives focus upon marketing information in defining a comprehensive mission, so must they focus upon the mission in decentralizing operations. Ultimately empowering by decentralizing operations is a test of maturity. The question for the executive is: "Can I keep my eye on the mission while keeping my hand on the operations?" This focus upon the centralized mission will enable executives to relate interdependently with other operations instead of being drawn into the "micro-dots" of daily performance.

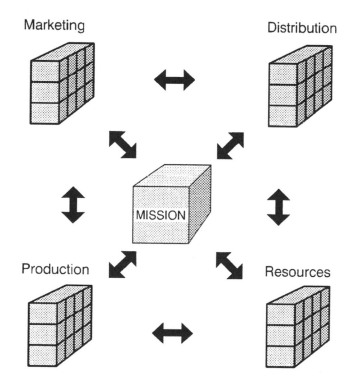

EMPOWERING OPERATIONS

The executive meaning of empowering operations is clear. The large companies that dominated world trade in durable goods and hardware are under great competitive pressure. As a consequence, they are getting leaner and more flexible. The Fortune 500 companies alone employed 2.2 million fewer people at the end of 1985 than they did at the beginning of 1980. They are subcontracting more. They are encouraging more leveraged buy-outs. The bigger, older companies are getting smaller. The ones that are still growing are creating new and decentralized operations in an attempt to maximize information processing and intrapreneurial initiative. At the same time, the newer kinds of companies are not getting very big. Like General Creech's operations, they are empowered naturally: as the "information press" becomes overwhelming, new and interdependent operations are broken out. The prospect of empowering operations by decentralizing is welcomed by executives, because they know that centralizing no longer works in an information society.

EXECUTIVE MEANING OF EMPOWERING BY DECENTRALIZING OPERATIONS

To sum, we may define operations in the Information Age as follows:

Operations are units of the organization that are empowered by decentralizing according to information
processing needs.

Committed to the centralized mission, then, the operations are decentralized according to their differentiated needs for infor-mation processing. The organizational goals become the opera-tion's mission as the units are empowered to achieve their objectives.

DECENTRALIZED OPERATIONS ⟶ MODIFIED OPERATIONS

THE DELTA TEAM

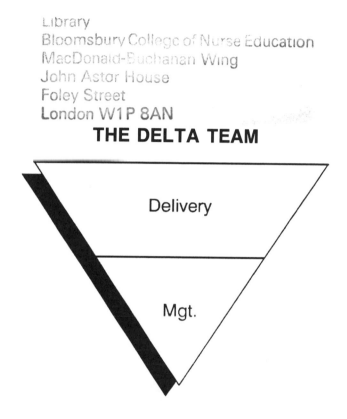

4. Modify and Invert Operations!

John Cannon is C.E.O. of Human Technology, Inc. Attuned to marketing information, the firm is constantly evolving to meet marketing needs. In terms of consumer information, the personnel are constantly searching for the subtle nuances in not only consumer needs but consumer uses: they are dedicated to making the consumers more productive. In terms of product information, they are concerned that the organization is always "state-of-the-art" in product innovation. In terms of sales information, the personnel use their interpersonal-based sales skills to keep their fingers on the pulse of our consumers. In short, Human Tech is driven by marketing information.

DRIVEN BY MARKETING INFORMATION

The first thing Cannon did organizationally was to bring the management staff together to define the central mission. The targets were clear for both private and public sector organizations. The goals were defined in terms of product-lines that emphasized services and products in instructional systems design (ISD) and management systems design (MSD). The strategies emphasized the resource, production, marketing, and distribution components for accomplishing the mission.

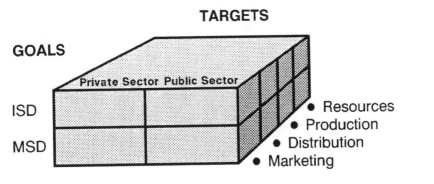

CENTRALIZING BY MISSION

The second thing that Cannon did organizationally was to decentralize by operations: research and development (R&D), publishing, and the differentiated private and public sector operations. The private and public sector operations serviced both management and personnel type target populations. The publishing served to disseminate products resulting from efforts of the other operations.

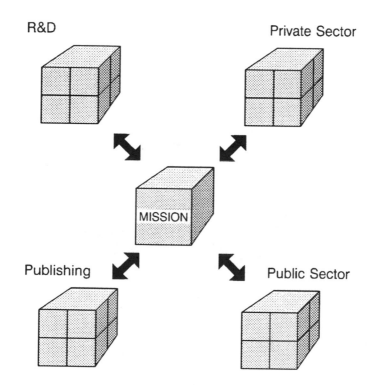

DECENTRALIZING OPERATIONS

The final thing that Cannon did in conjunction with the managers of the different operations was to develop delivery teams or "delta teams." In the illustration below, the public sector operations were modified and inverted in the following specialty areas: instructional systems design (ISD), management systems design (MSD), multi-media communications (MMC). Delta teams elevated the top delivery personnel by giving them both responsibility and authority for processing information directly with clients. In support of these delivery personnel, management staff were assigned to provide strategic support by resourcing and coordinating activities.

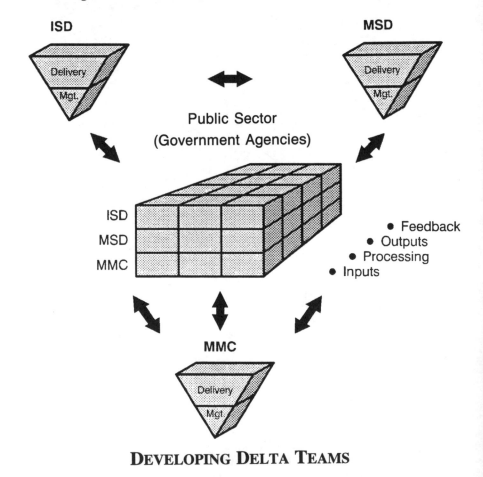

DEVELOPING DELTA TEAMS

To sum, Cannon followed all of the empowering principles: guiding by marketing information; centralizing by mission; decentralizing by operations; modifying and inverting operations. It remained for Cannon to work with staff and operations personnel to install programs to elevate the functioning of personnel in order to implement the operations. For Cannon, the results are clear: the organization has averaged nearly 100 percent growth per year over the last eight years.

"DOING SOMETHING RIGHT!"

64

"Modify and invert operations!" is the fourth strategy for economic growth. In the traditional organization of the Industrial Era, the personnel were organized in a hierarchical manner. Since information was relatively stable and unchanging, all critical data was cycled through the executives or policy makers. The executives processed the data and issued the mission statements and strategies that would direct the organization in an authoritarian manner. The managers transformed this information input into operations goals and systems for achieving the goals. In turn, supervisors processed objectives and programs, and production personnel performed the tasks and produced the products.

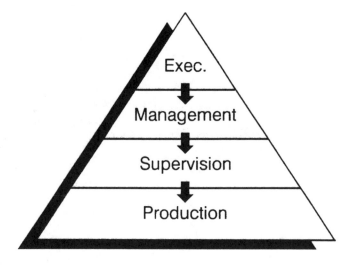

THE TRADITIONAL ORGANIZATION

During the Electronics Era, information became more complex and began to change more rapidly. By the time the information got through the layers of management to the executives, it lacked currency and accuracy. Moreover, the information had grown to an overwhelming size. Accordingly, the layers of management and supervision were reduced to more functional information processing roles. At the same time, production personnel were transformed into delivery personnel as production activities were automated and services were added to the product economy. Thus, the traditional hierarchical organization was transformed.

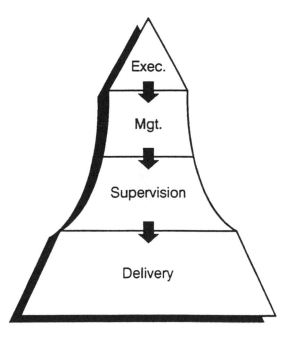

THE TRANSITIONAL ORGANIZATION

As information is not only changing but growing in complexity, the gap between management and delivery is being
closed. The supervisory function of operationalizing objectives
and programs is being incorporated in self-supervision by delivery personnel. In turn, the management personnel are cast in
more strategic support roles. At each of these levels, external
as well as internal, information relevant to the functions is
processed. Overall, the two-way information transactions between management and delivery personnel are intensified.

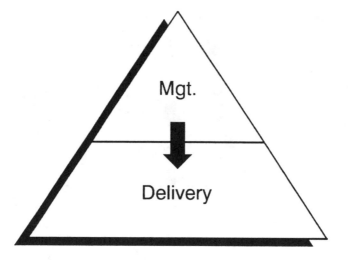

THE TRANSACTIONAL ORGANIZATION

In the information organization, the hierarchy is reversed and inverted in order to maximize information flow and processing. We label this inverted operation a delivery team or "delta team" because it maximizes the delivery of personnel and organizations. Those personnel who are at the point of greatest information pressure are assigned the processing responsibilities. Thus, the delivery personnel in all components are empowered and elevated in information processing responsibilities: salespersons in the marketplace become the greatest source of input for new product and service development; product developers intensify their processing of information as they increase their attempts to customize and tailor products to consumer needs; distribution and service personnel provide consumer feedback based upon their consumer interactions; trainers and other personnel process information to maximize their support of other components. At the same time, management is empowered at a strategic level: those personnel who are most experienced in designing the immediate strategies required to achieve the long-range mission are empowered in discharging the support functions of strategic decision-making and systems planning.

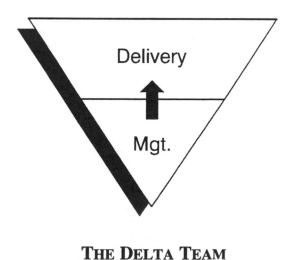

THE DELTA TEAM

By default if not by intention, executives can no longer control or process information. We have already empowered managers in information processing. It remains for us to empower all personnel in information processing. To do this, we need to invert and elevate the roles of both delivery and management personnel. In effect, the information environment is requiring a higher calibre information processor "on the line" where all the action is taking place. By selection or, more likely, by training, executives need to establish policy to "make the little people into big people." These are the policy decisions that account for huge chunks of variance in organizational productivity. The prospect of modifying operations is experienced with urgency by executives because the future of the organizations depend upon these modifications.

EXECUTIVE MEANING OF EMPOWERING BY INVERTING OPERATIONS

Thus, centralized by mission and decentralized by operations, the information organization maximizes information flow and processing. In short, it gives the processing responsibilities to the personnel at the point of greatest flow. The delivery team or "delta team" is the organization of the future:

> The delta team is a decentralized unit that is inverted to maximize the information processing of those personnel at the point of greatest information flow.

Obviously, in order to discharge these responsibilities, the functioning of both delivery and management personnel must be empowered by human processing.

INVERTING OPERATIONS ⟶ HUMAN PROCESSING

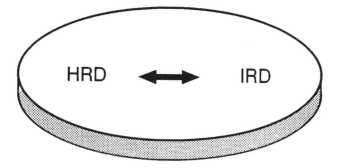

5. Emphasize Human Processing!

Four years ago, Springfield Remanufacturing Center Corporation (SRC) was a division of International Harvester Co., a rebuilder of engines and engine components. It was also losing $2 million a year on sales of $26 million when Jack Stack arrived. In 1983, Stack and 123 other employees bought the business from Harvester. The story of how a dying division of Harvester became one of America's most competitive companies is the story of "The Great Game of Business." (Rhodes and Amend, 1986)

THE DOWNTURN

Gamesmanship is Stack's guiding concept. For Stack, business is essentially a game—albeit a very serious one. If the team is going to win the game, then the players must learn to play the game. First, they must understand the rules. Second, they must receive all of the information they need to follow the action. Third, they must have the opportunity to win or lose. Stack has gone to great lengths to involve every employee in "The Great Game of Business." To this end he has developed three major program thrusts: education, information and incentives.

"THE GREAT GAME OF BUSINESS"

First, Stack designed an extraordinary education program to teach the employees how the Game is played. Every worker in the plant had an opportunity to take a series of courses covering most elements of business curriculum ranging from accounting to warehousing. More recently, the company has organized an ongoing management training program aimed at opening up opportunities for employee advancement. If the education program is calculated to involve personnel in the Game, then the information program is dedicated to maintaining employee involvement in the Game.

PROGRAM 1—EDUCATION

Recognizing that quantitative management can be toxic to humans, Stack set about to develop his information program. The intent of the information program is to transform a rigorous, obsessive, quantitative regimen into personally meaningful numbers for the employees. For example, the electronic message board is constantly informing employees of their positioning in the game. "Fuel injection labor utilization 98%" means that the fuel injection pump assemblers spent 98 percent of their time on direct labor rather than overhead during the first half of their shift. If they maintained such a pace, they become eligible for involvement in the third program—incentives. In short, the information program is calculated to maintain the maximum involvement created by education. Indeed, Stack is convinced that his numbers-crunching works so well because his people are so involved.

PROGRAM 2—INFORMATION

*The **STP—GUTR** program is an acronym for "Stop the Praise—Give Us a Raise." The electronic ticker merely tells the employees how well they are doing in the incentive program, the third leg of the Great Game. Instead of funneling a predetermined percentage of profits into a bonus pool, **SRC** ties its bonuses to the achievement of specific goals. In 1985, for example, there were two such goals: 1) to increase operating income from 6 percent to 15 percent of sales; 2) to control costs by reducing the plant's overhead from $39 to $32 per hour. Although the charge-out rate was eventually cut to $23 per hour, the company missed its operating income objective. As a consequence, employees received bonuses of 7.8 percent of gross salary rather than the 10 percent they would have earned had the company met both goals. Stack comments:*

> *"It's like a big read board at Caesar's Palace. You know, the one with 10 or 15 games on it, for any sport you want to bet on. The odds are constantly changing and the action is fantastic."*

PROGRAM 3—INCENTIVES

*The results are also fantastic. Since the leveraged buy-out,
SRC's sales have grown 40 percent per year to $42 million in
1986. Net operating income has risen to 11 percent. The debt-
to-equity ratio has been cut from 89-to-1 to 5-to-1. The ap-
praised value of a share in the company's employee stock
ownership plan has increased from 10 cents to $8.45. On the
human front, absenteeism and employee turnover have disappeared and accident rates have fallen dramatically. Stack sum-
marizes his philosophy behind "The Great Game of Business:"*

> *"Look, we're appealing to the highest level thinking we
> can in every employee in our company. Why hire a guy
> and use his brains to grind a crankshaft?"*

THE TURNAROUND

"Emphasize human processing!" is the fifth strategy for economic growth. In the Industrial Age raw materials were transformed into finished products by mechanical processing. As may be noted, capital machinery and labor supplemented the inputs; supervisory monitoring controlled the processing; and results information dominated the feedback. Together, these were the primary ingredients of the product-based industrial economy.

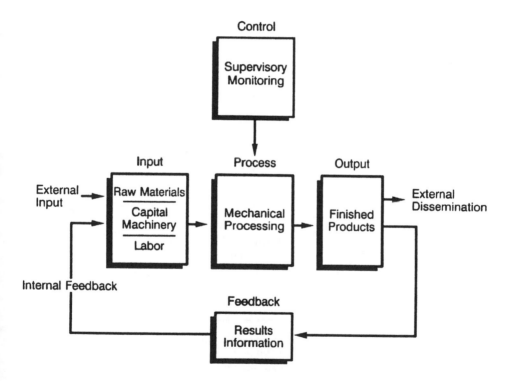

ORGANIZATIONAL PROCESSING IN THE INDUSTRIAL AGE

During the Electronics Era, human and information resources evolved as critical inputs; computer processing ascended over mechanical processing; controls were eased with the introduction of participative management methods and the monitoring of outputs rather than processes; services became important outputs; productivity information on both results outputs and resource inputs constituted feedback. To sum, these were the primary ingredients of the so-called service economy.

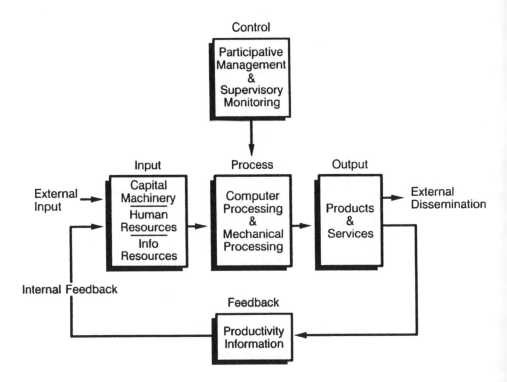

**ORGANIZATIONAL PROCESSING IN THE
ELECTRONICS ERA**

In the Information Age, human and information resources dominate resource inputs; human processing dominates processing; concern with consumer benefits complements product and service outputs; feedback is provided on individual performance as well as consumer and producer productivity. To sum, these are the ingredients of an evolving information economy.

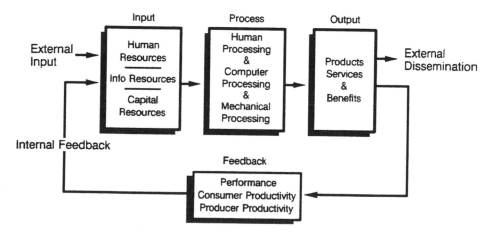

ORGANIZATIONAL PROCESSING IN THE AGE OF INFORMATION

From an organizational perspective, we may view human processing as the synergistic relationship between human- and information-resource development (HRD ↔ IRD). In such a synergistic interaction, each element grows as the other grows. Thus, human resource development contributes to stimulating the growth of information resource development. Conversely, as information grows, it contributes to the development of human resources. We can see these ingredients most clearly in the individual thinking, interpersonal processing and organizational functioning of personnel: they process productive information and, in turn, are impacted by it. These ingredients of human processing in interaction with each other hold the keys to improved productivity in the Age of Information.

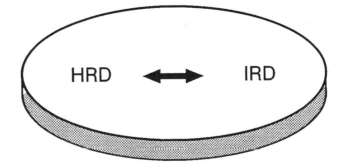

THE FUNCTIONS OF HUMAN PROCESSING

The net effect of human processing is empowering personnel. Personnel are empowered, not by authorizing alone, but by skilling and then authorizing them to use the skills. To share power by authorizing—without skilling—is an empty gesture to improving productivity. To authorize people who have been skilled in human processing is the single most potent source of improving productivity. In short, there is no empowering without skilling in human processing. Put another way, human processing is the prepotent source of empowering both personnel and organizations in the Age of Information.

EMPOWERING PERSONNEL

For executives, the meaning of empowering personnel by human processing is profound! The human processing of information is the greatest source of economic productivity growth in the Age of the New Capitalism. Under the guidance of personnel who are thinking productively, the "numbers-crunching" potential of computer processing can finally contribute significantly to organizational productivity. It is to be emphasized that the corporate environment must support human processing. Like Jack Stack and the *SRC*, the implementation of a human processing intervention will be based upon three critical programs: 1) education; 2) information; 3) incentives. The principle of empowering personnel by human processing is exciting for executive personnel because it promises to free the executives, themselves, to process.

EXECUTIVE MEANING OF HUMAN PROCESSING

In summary, empowering personnel through human processing skills is the single most important ingredient in empowering organizations in the Age of the New Capitalism:

> Human processing is the systematic transformation of the raw data of human experience into productive information of operational utility.

In short, human processing is productive thinking—individually, interpersonally, organizationally. Indeed, human processing enables the organization to empower itself: processing marketing information to centralize the mission; processing operational information to decentralize and modify the operations. Human processing brings with it its own set of requirements, first and foremost of which is skilling the personnel in the processing skills which enable them to "think better."

HUMAN PROCESSING ⟶ "THINKING BETTER"

THINKING SKILLS

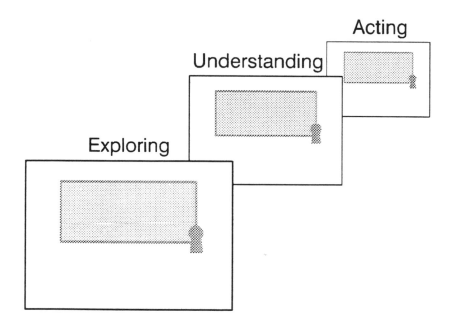

6. Think Better!

I have the distinct privilege of being a policy-making executive in an Information Age agency. We are an R&D firm committed to putting technology in the service of humanity. In the process, we are attempting to accomplish not only a human and technological interface; we are committed to creating a "critical mass"—or synergy—within and between the humans and their technologies. The project contents may range from state-of-the-art human and information resource development and management systems such as the expert systems of artificial intelligence through multimedia systems (including computer-assisted instruction) to differentiated productivity designs based upon increasingly futuristic scenarios. Over the past five years, we have implemented about eight hundred new projects, more than two hundred in the past year, so that we are averaging one new project for every working day in the year. Every week there are dozens of iterations of informational input and feedback, the most significant of which are fielded by our chief executive officer. Of these messages, perhaps a dozen may change the direction of any one of our projects from 1° to 180°. At least one message per week may change the direction of our entire agency from 1° to 180°. Indeed, we live on the razor's edge, poised between growth and extinction.

HUMAN CONDITIONING AND HUMAN CRISIS

In my experience, by far the great majority of humans are
conditioned responders. *As such, they limit the information they
receive to the wavelengths with which they feel comfortable.
For them, it is like setting the dial of their radios or television
sets to one particular station. They allow themselves to receive
only that input for which they have a response. Or, they make
the same response over and over regardless of the informational
input. Clearly, these personnel are most effective in dependent
roles where they are handed tasks or steps in a program to perform based upon goals determined by others. Because of there
inability to "compute" the constantly changing information
requirements imposed by the environment, they tend to produce low
quality products—late. Ultimately, the* **conditioned responders**
*are counterproductive, because their limited response reper-
toires force them to consume increasing levels of resource
inputs while producing decreasing levels of results outputs. The
great paradox is that the* **conditioned responders** *who avoid or
distort the information input to serve their conditioned comfort
zones are often very unhappy people. They become aversively
conditioned to any information input that does not converge
with the responses they already have. They say, "Don't teach
me anything I don't already know!" The* **conditioned responders**
*are the dinosaurs of the Information Age. They are increasingly
isolated as they teeter precariously on the edge of extinction.*

CONDITIONED RESPONDERS

*A minority of personnel—perhaps 10 percent or 20 percent—
fall into the category of **participative learners**. They participate
in the learning process. They are most effective in considering
alternative courses of action to achieve goals, once the data has
been analyzed, factored and synthesized. When performing on
these terms, **participative learners** can contribute to the definition and achievement of goals. Generally, they produce products of acceptable quality—on time. Although they participate in
defining their own goals, ultimately the **participative learners**
may become unproductive, due to their lack of comprehensive
responsiveness. Today, the **participative learners**, nourished as
they were by the participative styles of learning and management of the last twenty years, are becoming increasingly
anxiety-ridden. They are beginning to recognize the inadequacy
of their responses. They do not process the iterations of input
and feedback to shape tailored products with maximum effectiveness and efficiency. They are made **most** anxious by the
processors who do process. The participative learners are
brought to constant states of crises and tension by the information press. Whether or not they can develop the necessary
variability in their learning styles will decide the survival of
their species.*

PARTICIPATIVE LEARNERS

*Less than 5 percent of the personnel—the **processors**—elicit and expand their information inputs and sources, process the information by factoring the significant contributions of the information, and then dedicate their processing toward incrementally greater productivity. Not only are they tolerant of the information press, they are committed to expanding its size and variability. They don't just endure the iterations of processing, they enjoy the creative negotiation of their values with any implied requirements of the information. Not only do they subscribe verbally to performance improvement, they increase their productivity exponentially with every iteration of the production cycle, producing accelerating results outputs while investing decelerating resource inputs. The **processors** begin to experience information inputs as a "high." The more input, the more brain activity. The more brain activity, the more "critical mass" of thinking. The more thinking, the more productivity! They are the creators of the Information Age. Their information by-products incessantly move the Age toward its mission: information processing for human benefits. Happy and fulfilled, they are increasingly synergistic as they move toward their personal mission: to grow, to become, to fulfill their goals.*

HUMAN PROCESSORS

"Think better!" is the sixth strategy for economic growth. Throughout the history of humankind, we have never been asked to think or process. Until now! Through the Industrial Age, we were only asked to make conditioned, "knee-jerk" type responses. Conditioned responses (R) are specific responses reinforced by association and reward to specific stimuli (S). Parents conditioned children; teachers, students; bosses, workers. The assumption was that the more experienced person processed the more accurate and effective response. In this context, our families were centered upon ceremonial initiations, our schools upon ritualistic memorization, our industries upon formalized apprenticeships. These approaches serviced us so long as the information upon which they were predicated changed slowly—ever so slowly.

S → R

CONDITIONING

With the advent of the Electronics Era and the increasing quantity and complexity of its information, the processing approaches shifted. Specific conditioned responses no longer sufficed. What was needed was a repertoire or series of responses upon which to draw. Accordingly, the human being intervened between stimulus and response. The human was the repository of responses. With a hierarchy of responses, we could discriminate specific stimuli and emit appropriate responses. It was like learning to hit a baseball by swinging level (a la Charlie Lau), up (Ted Williams), or down (Carl Yastrzemski). Armed with such a repertoire of hitting responses, the batter could emit the appropriate response to stimulus conditions. Discriminating stimuli and responses still did not require thinking but rather merely amassing responses. That is why parenting was dominated by the "edge system," teaching by sharing responses to be "learned," and working by participative management and quality circles.

$$\mathbf{S} \rightarrow \begin{array}{ccc} S_1 & \rightarrow & R_1 \\ S_{...} & \rightarrow & R_{...} \\ S_n & \rightarrow & R_n \end{array} \rightarrow \mathbf{R}$$

LEARNING

It was not until the Information Age that human processing or thinking was required. Thinking involves creating entirely new responses. Indeed, thinking may involve creating entirely new stimuli. Thinking skills enable us to transform the raw data of human experience into productive information, i.e., information can be acted upon. Thinking skills put us in charge of our own destinies. In thinking, we naturally go through three phases. First, we explore our experience in order to know where we are. Second, we understand our goals in order to know where we want or need to be. Third, we act to achieve our goals by moving from where we are to where we want or need to be.

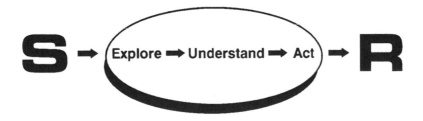

THINKING

For example, a helpful way to conceive of one kind of thinking, systems thinking, is in terms of processing information through three doors. The key to these doors is knowing our mission and its strategic goals and objectives. This knowledge enables us to factor the relevant information to be processed. It also allows us to assess our level of goal achievement. In the first phase, we explore our experience by analyzing our current operating systems. In the second phase, we understand our goals by synthesizing new and more productive systems. In the third phase, we act by operationalizing objectives and programs to implement our systems and achieve our goals.

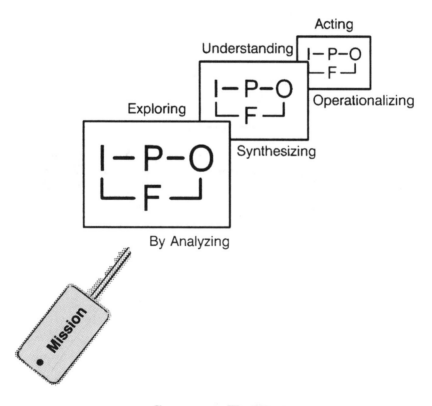

SYSTEMS THINKING

Systems are the operations we develop to achieve our goals. In exploring, then, we analyze current operating systems. We analyze the human information and capital resource inputs; the individual, interpersonal, and organizational processing; the response, product, and service outputs; and the performance, production, and delivery feedback. At the executive level, the feedback also evaluates producer and consumer benefits.

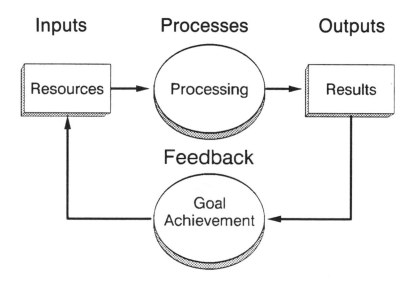

EXPLORING BY ANALYZING SYSTEMS

The magic of systems thinking occurs in the understanding phase. First, we expand the alternative systems and operations within systems. Then we narrow to the preferred system or operations. We narrow by evaluating the systems and operations in terms of their ability to achieve our goals productively. We then synthesize a new and more productive operating system which enables us to achieve improved goals.

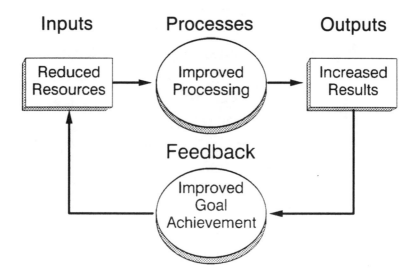

UNDERSTANDING BY SYNTHESIZING SYSTEMS

Finally, we act by operationalizing the systems. First, we define the objectives within each of the operations. Next, we develop the programs to achieve these operational objectives. Operationalizing the systems in this manner makes the objectives and, thus, the systems goals achievable.

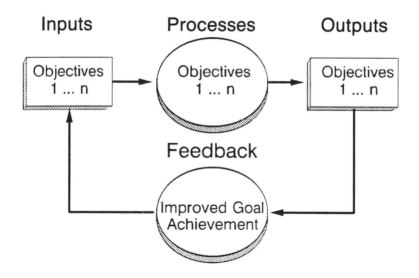

ACTING BY OPERATIONALIZING SYSTEMS

Ultimately, all power is derived from thinking. Human capital is the source of the "next idea." Information capital is the operations that implement the "last idea." Together, human and information capital account for 85 percent of the variance in economic productivity growth. Developing human resources—primarily through thinking skills training—is the source of human capital and, indirectly, information capital. The real power in the Age of Information is the ability to process that information—thinking!

THINKING POWER

For the executive, "thinking better" is everything! In the Age of Information, empowering means skills. We empower people when we teach them to think for themselves. When personnel are empowered to think in an organization, they dedicate their thinking to implementing or, indeed, eliminating their roles. When personnel are skilled, they are empowered to relate all of their tasks to achieving the mission. Empowering by skilling is a relief for executives because it helps to remove a burden of processing they can no longer execute.

EXECUTIVE MEANING OF "THINKING BETTER"

To sum, human processing is achieved by thinking skills:

> Productive thinking skills enable people to transform
> their current systems and operations into productive
> systems and operations by exploring, understanding,
> and acting upon the systems.

Clearly, in order to accomplish our goals and missions in more
productive ways, we need to complement our individual thinking with interpersonal processing.

"THINKING BETTER" ⟶ "RELATING FULLY"

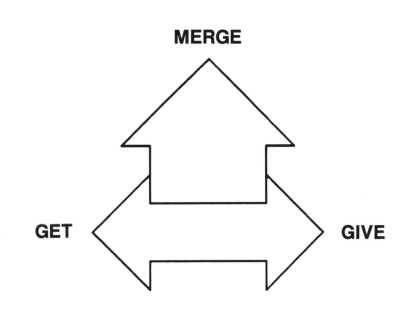

MERGE

GET

GIVE

7. Relate Fully!

Nothing is worse in business than a government contractor getting a "Method D" evaluation. It means that the quality of the contractor's products is poor. It is the last stage before termination of the contract. It calls for drastic production measures. In one such case, the contractor called in a number of systems engineers and "troubleshooters," and also summoned Bill Grace, a general foreman at another plant in the corporation. The systems engineers saw the problem in the systems designs. The "troubleshooters" found the problems in the implementation of the design. Grace found the problem in the tube bending process. A part was being produced at a lower tolerance than was acceptable. Consequently, the production-line workers would not get the appropriate "crimp" and the part was leaking all over. Several activities followed. The systems designers and "troubleshooters" went home. Grace worked with the personnel to devise a new method for "harnessing" the part. Shortly thereafter, the "Method D" was lifted.

TROUBLESHOOTING

What makes Grace unique? For one thing, the enormous productivity of his operations. Alone, he documented nearly $2,000,000 in cost avoidance savings over a two-year performance management study. In other words, Grace sets the exemplary standard. What makes Grace tick? Physically, he has enormous energy and stamina. Emotionally, he has been described as a happy, "blue-collar" type. Intellectually, he is technically proficient and without conflict in going after rational goals. But the thing that distinguishes Grace from all other managers at his level is his ability to process interpersonally. Grace shares his concerns with his personnel; he compares their images with his; he negotiates a convergence of the images; he works with the personnel to plan to improve the performance. When they perform their tasks, the personnel feel that their frames of reference have been taken into consideration, the tasks defined in operational terms, and the performance planned in doable steps. The personnel who work under him love him as one of their own. He relates on a daily basis to all of the personnel in his plant. He shares all relevant information with them and involves them in the decision-making process. Even with such delicate installations as robotry, he involves his personnel in the process. Consequently, Grace never has any grievances filed against him.

INTERPERSONAL LEADERSHIP

*The thing that empowered Bill Grace as an exemplary manager was General Dynamics' new interpersonal skills program. In the persons and skills of Todd Holder and Jack Shultz, his trainers, he found the answer to the problems of crises management which had plagued and, indeed, dominated him and other managers. Instead of "Give and Go," the managers learned to "Get, Give, Merge and Go." This interpersonal relating process required them to **get** the employees' images of the task, **give** or share their own images, negotiate a **merge** or convergence of the images of the goal if there were discrepancies, and work with the employees to develop a program. The employees would then **go** on to plan and implement the program to achieve the goal.*

INTERPERSONAL RELATING

Most important for our purposes, these managers found that when they made the front-end investment of sharing and converging images of tasks, they received the concomitant benefits of improved performance. Under the old "Give and Go" order, crises often grew steadily and cumulatively because of gaps in employee and/or managerial understanding of specific tasks. Under the "Get, Give, Merge and Go" program, managers like Bill Grace found that they were preventively reducing or eliminating crises because both they and the employees understood the tasks.

INTERPERSONAL PROCESSING

"Relate fully!" is the seventh strategy for economic growth. Through the Industrial Age, conditioned responding dominated all human endeavors. Simply stated, a stimulus was presented and a response was evoked. Through a process of association and reinforcement, people were conditioned to emit the responses upon the presentation of the stimuli. Children learned the family or church code by rote, learners memorized grammar or multiplication tables, and workers imitated the performances of others by repetition and reinforcement. Interpersonally, all that was needed from the controller—the parent, teacher or boss—was to direct the presentation of the stimulus and control the emission of the response. In business and industry, we are most familiar with the directing and controlling as the supervisory process.

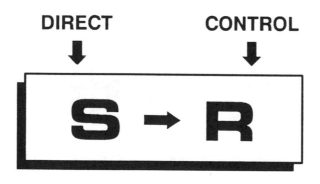

CONTROLLING

With the changing and growing information requirements of the Electronics Era came the recognition that the controller does not have all the answers. With this recognition, the interpersonal role was shifted to a more facilitative one. Instead of directing the stimulus and controlling the response, the other person facilitated the process. Whether assuming or training a response repertoire or hierarchy, parents, teachers, and supervisors alike facilitated the other person's discrimination of the stimuli and performance of the appropriate response.

**ATTENDING
&
RESPONDING**

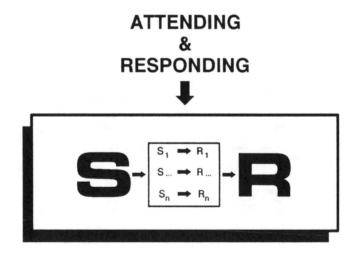

RELATING

With the entry into the Information Age, the information requirements intensified, and with them came the recognition of the need for more egalitarian interpersonal relationships. Now it is assumed that neither party, or none of the participants, has the answer. Consequently, all parties process individually ($S \rightarrow P \rightarrow R$) before processing interpersonally. The helpers or supervisors share by first getting and then giving their images of the responses, usually in the form of goals or problems. Finally, they negotiate merged images of the responses before going on to plan the achievement of the objectives involved.

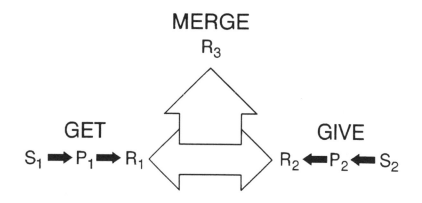

PROCESSING

For example, to continue the example of systems processing, the initiator at any level—executive, manager, or supervisor—first responds to get the image of the goals or problems. These images are most productively communicated in terms of the operations of the systems involved: inputs, processes, outputs, feedback (I-P-0-F).

RESPONDING TO GET IMAGES

After responding to get images, it is most productive to communicate one's own image. Our own image is communicated in the same manner as the ones we elicited, i.e., in terms of the operations of the systems involved. Again, in relation to individual thinking, personnel may initiate to give the products of their exploring, understanding and acting.

INITIATING TO GIVE IMAGES

Finally, after getting and giving, it is most productive to merge images. That way, the images of all parties converge upon the same goals and problems. We merge by jointly negotiating the most productive operations, i.e., those that have the most leverage in achieving our goals and resolving our problems.

NEGOTIATING TO MERGE IMAGES

The power of interpersonal processing is found in adding value to individual processing. For example, we like to think of relating as illustrated below. I respond to get "your way" or your image. I initiate to give "my way" or my image. We negotiate to merge images to go "our way." However, "our way" is not a compromised and neutralized version of the other images. Rather, it yields the "high way," a "values added" image of productive interpersonal processing.

The High Way

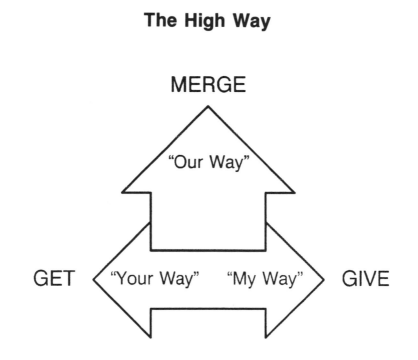

RELATING POWER

Along with thinking, interdependent relating is the cornerstone of the Age of Information. Interdependency is a term to describe both our independency and our dependency. Our independency is defined by our individual thinking skills. Our interdependency upon one another is defined by our interpersonal processing skills. Interpersonal processing is simply thinking out loud with someone else. It is of greatest value after the participants have engaged in thinking individually. If we are to maximize the human processing of information, then we must emphasize the two great sources of human processing—individual and interpersonal processing. To discover the productive thinking that people can do by themselves is a personal joy. To discover, as Bill Grace does, the productive thinking that people can do with each other is a celebration of our humanity.

EXECUTIVE MEANING OF "RELATING FULLY"

In this manner, interpersonal as well as individual processing is maximized in the decentralized delivery operations:

> Productive interpersonal processing involves adding
> value to productive information produced by the fol-
> lowing procedures:
> - Getting the others' images
> - Giving one's own image
> - Merging images

Interpersonal processing in synergy with individual thinking
accounts for most improvements in individual performance and
organizational productivity. In short, individual thinking in conjunction with interpersonal processing prepares us for "working
smarter" in discharging our organizational functions.

"RELATING FULLY" ⟶ **"WORKING SMARTER"**

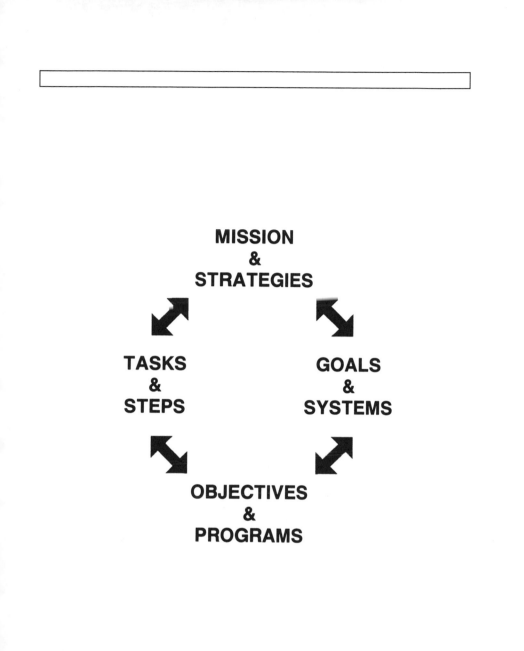

MISSION
&
STRATEGIES

TASKS
&
STEPS

GOALS
&
SYSTEMS

OBJECTIVES
&
PROGRAMS

8. Work Smarter!

T.C. was the director of a state agency (Kaplan, 1983). His word-processing workload was growing so fast that it was becoming an obstacle to discharging the agency's responsibilities. The processors were simply unable to deal effectively with the burgeoning paperwork. T.C. analyzed the resources. Among other things he found that the current keyboard, the QWERTY keyboard, was designed to be inefficient and to slow down the user. Yes, that is correct: to slow down the user! The reason this was done was because fifty years ago, typists had been going too fast and they were jamming the manual machines. Frequency of use of letters in the English language had been determined and the most-used letters were separated to all four keyboard centers. Typists were forced constantly to reach up and down for letters, and this reaching curtailed their speed in typing.

"Slowing Down the Users"

T.C. rediscovered the Dvorak keyboard, which had been designed in the early 1940s, prior to electronic equipment. The Dvorak keyboard required less finger action in reaching the desired letters. The most-used letters—vowels and the frequent consonants—were situated in the "house row" directly under the typist's fingers. The Dvorak keyboard appealed to T.C. because of its potential for increased productivity as well as ease of use. T.C. set up an extensive program to introduce the new system, train the personnel, and install and implement the new keyboard.

"SPEEDING UP THE USERS"

After an initial decrease in productivity, the Dvorak workers were able to produce 60 percent to 80 percent more work than using the QWERTY system. Furthermore, they were able to do so while reducing staff size. In straight salary terms, the new system produced results benefits calculated at $150,000 annually. In addition, employee turnover and medical expenses were reduce significantly. Most important for T.C.'s purposes, his agency was able to keep pace with the steadily increasing workload. Its clientele was served at the highest level and on time.

PERFORMANCE IMPROVEMENT

The story of the Dvorak keyboard is important from a number of perspectives. In one response, it simply was an idea whose time had come. It did not require great processing skills to analyze existing technology and search for alternatives. The Dvorak keyboard is important because of what did not happen over the last two decades of the Hardware Age. Given the electronic capacity, millions of typists spent billions of hours typing unquestioningly on a keyboard designed for another age. By T.C.'s calculations alone, we may calculate a loss of 50 percent or more of productive capacity.

LOST PRODUCTIVITY

"Work smarter!" is the eighth strategy for economic growth. For example, in the Industrial Age, the executive's processing burdens, while many, relied upon a relatively constant and unchanging data base. Thus, the executive received and processed the entire data. In this manner, the executive produced the orders and directions that were passed down to others in a hierarchical way. The thinking process was linear and straightforward: most often a continuation of slowly changing policy. Thus, the slowly changing data base was transformed into slowly changing missions and strategies by ill-defined policy-making procedures.

EXECUTIVE DIMENSIONS

Today, in the Age of Information, we have operational images of the functions of policy making: mission development and strategic plans. The product of mission development is a mission: targets, goals, strategies that drive the organization. In turn, strategic planning defines the organizational dimensions which enable the accomplishment of the mission. These operational policy-making skills define the creative executive's contribution in the Age of Information.

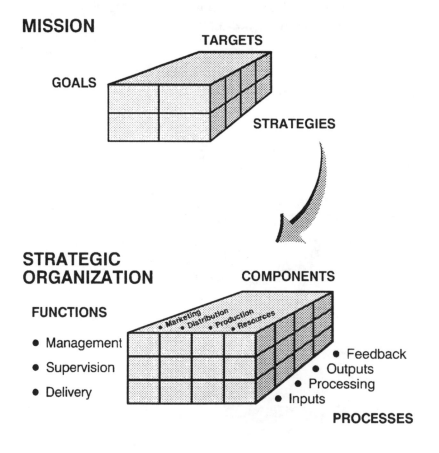

OPERATIONAL EXECUTIVE DIMENSIONS

The operations may, in turn, be decentralized and modified. Within these operations, then, the management functions emphasize transforming the executive missions and strategies into operational goals. Operational goals are observable and measurable goals emphasizing the production of products and the delivery of benefits. These goals may be measured quantitatively by such indices as volume, rate, and timeliness. They may also be measured qualitatively by indices such as functionality, accuracy, and creativity.

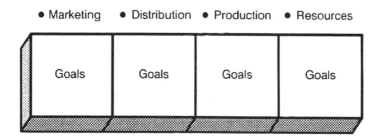

● Marketing   ● Distribution   ● Production   ● Resources

| Goals | Goals | Goals | Goals |

MANAGEMENT FUNCTIONS

Having defined the operational goals, the managers' primary function remains planning the systems needed to achieve the goals and then providing strategic support to the implementors of the system—the delivery personnel. The basic processing system transforms resource inputs into results outputs. The level of goal achievement is evaluated and fed back as information input into the processing system. In order to implement modified operations, then, managers will need the critical information processing skills to discharge management functions: defining and measuring goals; planning systems to achieve the goals.

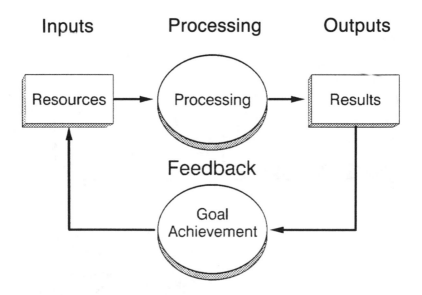

MANAGEMENT SYSTEMS

In turn, supervisory functions emphasize transforming the management goals and systems into objectives. These functions may be incorporated within the delivery functions. Objectives are defined by the operations needed to accomplish them as illustrated below.

OPERATIONS	DEFINITIONS
Components --	Parts or Participants
Functions --	Activities or Uses
Procedures --	Methods or Mechanics
Conditions --	Content or Environment
Standards --	Achievement or Excellence

SUPERVISORY OBJECTIVES

Finally, the delivery functions emphasize transforming the supervisory objectives and programs into operational tasks. Operational tasks are defined behaviorally in terms of the skills, knowledge and attitudes performed.

Skills — Things we do or behaviors we perform
Knowledge — Things we know which support performance
Attitudes — Things we feel that support performance

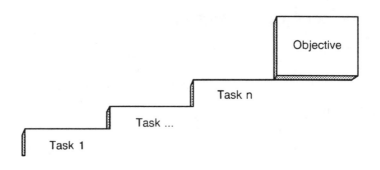

DELIVERY TASKS

In short, the ingredients of productive processing are individual, interpersonal and organizational processing. These
processing ingredients serve to transform the raw data of human
experience into productive and usable information. These
processing ingredients enable human productivity.

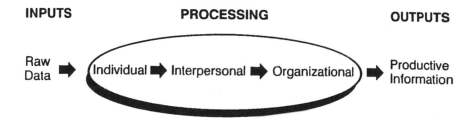

THE INGREDIENTS OF HUMAN PROCESSING

We may view individual, interpersonal, and organizational processing at the various levels of functions within an organization. Together, the individual, interpersonal, and organizational processing skills account for the process of "working smarter," which empowers us to contribute to economic productivity growth. "Working smarter" is working power.

WORKING SMARTER

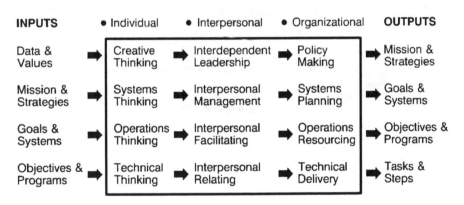

PROCESSING

INPUTS	• Individual	• Interpersonal	• Organizational	OUTPUTS
Data & Values	Creative Thinking	Interdependent Leadership	Policy Making	Mission & Strategies
Mission & Strategies	Systems Thinking	Interpersonal Management	Systems Planning	Goals & Systems
Goals & Systems	Operations Thinking	Interpersonal Facilitating	Operations Resourcing	Objectives & Programs
Objectives & Programs	Technical Thinking	Interpersonal Relating	Technical Delivery	Tasks & Steps

WORKING POWER

For executives, there are many personal meanings to "working smarter."

- *Growth* is an idea in the brain and not a number on the balance sheet!
- *Capital* is an idea that exists in a person's head or on paper!
- *Security* is our next good idea!
- *Career* is your last good idea!
- *Management* is finding people with ideas and keeping your "hands off" rather than on!

In short, "working smarter" implies "thinking better" and "relating fully." The essential task of the executive is to learn to "work smarter" and then enable the personnel, beginning with management, to "work smarter." The executive does this by incorporating individual thinking, interpersonal processing, and organizational functioning skills programs into the educational experience of the personnel. It is exhilarating for executives to understand that what makes us most productive also makes us most human—our minds!

THE EXECUTIVE MEANING OF "WORKING SMARTER"

To sum, organizational functioning in decentralized delivery operations is maximized by "working smarter":

> "Working smarter" is defined by the products of in-
> dividual thinking and interpersonal processing insured
> by planning to discharge organizational functions.

Together, individual, interpersonal, and organizational process-ing account for "working smarter" and prepare us for intra-preneurial initiatives that lead to improvements in organizational productivity.

"WORKING SMARTER" ⟶ FREEING INITIATIVE

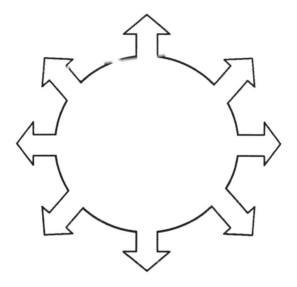

9. Free Initiative!

Sharon Fisher was finding her way in the corporation. She had been hired a few brief years ago in a clerical capacity on a computer systems design project. She found herself surrounded by many high-powered personnel, mostly men and mostly products of postgraduate education. While Fisher herself had a bachelor's degree, she stood in awe of the "heavies" around her. Systematically, through evidence of competence, she worked her way to higher and higher-level tasks. Soon she was assigned management responsibilities for entire projects.

"WORKING HER WAY UP"

Fisher always focused upon designing the project to meet customer needs. She did not let her own feelings enter in except to produce the best possible project. She front-end loaded on information in order to reduce her investment of resources in the project. She not only "worked harder" (which she did) and "thought harder" (which she also did), she gradually learned to "think better." She began to emphasize efficiency and effectiveness in both process and product. She wanted to produce the best commercial product to meet the customer's image. At the same time, she replaced resource expenditures with a factoring process that emphasized the "mini-max" principle: minimum resources for maximum results. By these very criteria, Fisher herself began to outproduce other personnel. She simply did "more with less."

"PRODUCING MORE WITH LESS"

The data was reflected in her "fast track" promotions. Year after year, she herself delivered more dollars worth of projects than anyone else in the corporation. With the exception of one of the core delivery personnel, she delivered products and services on twice as many dollars as anyone else (she was more than 50 percent higher than that one delivery specialist). In addition, she managed more production than any of the management personnel. Again, she accounted for more than double the dollar average overall, although two of the management personnel approached her numbers. Finally, because of her success in management and delivery as well as her disposition toward commercializing her products, she was also the leading marketer in the corporation. Here she accounted for approximately 10 percent of the gross sales of the corporation, more than doubling the average of the marketing personnel.

INCREASING PRODUCTIVITY RATIOS

140

The decision makers involved with Fisher were faced with the fundamental organizational issue of exemplarship:

"How do we organize to maximize exposure while at the same time maximizing productivity?"

Typically and traditionally, the exemplars are reassigned to a supervisory or management role. This defies productivity logic: the delivery person extraordinaire is assigned to directing the delivery person ordinaire. In most cases, it will be years—if ever—before the exemplar can emerge from the management maze to contribute to organizational productivity. Basically, by making the management assignment, we are indeed sacrificing the one for the many: the one who outproduces the sum total of the others will now supervise others.

MAXIMIZING EXPOSURE TO EXEMPLARS

What the decision makers did instead was to develop a fundamental organizational assumption from which a series of organizational propositions were derived. The fundamental organizational assumption was this:

"We maximize organizational productivity by maximizing support for the exemplar and learning for the other personnel."

In other words, there are two tracks with organizational implications: 1) mobilize all necessary resources to free the exemplar to achieve still higher levels of productivity, i.e., "Turn her loose!"; 2) maximize the learning of the other personnel from direct exposure to the exemplar. An understanding of the changing organizational dimensions made these assumptions and propositions possible.

ORGANIZING AROUND EXEMPLARS

The decision makers were committed to maximizing Fisher's exemplary performance. At the same time, they wanted to upgrade the performance of others. Accordingly, they designed an organization to free Fisher's intrapreneurial initiative. First, they implemented the "Delta Team" concept, inverting delivery and management responsibilities with Fisher in the delivery role. Second, they provided strategic support for her efforts. Third, they freed her to organize her own exemplary delivery unit. In short, the decision makers configured the entire organization around freeing Fisher's intrapreneurial initiative.

MAXIMIZING INITIATIVE

"Free initiative" is the ninth strategy for economic growth. The single most difficult human dimension to learn and, therefore, to teach is initiative. Initiative involves assuming a new direction. Initiative may be described in a variety of ways: "Throwing out a skyhook," "pulling oneself up by one's bootstraps," "making something out of nothing." Above all, initiative requires physical courage because the initiator is "putting it on the line." It takes a special kind of executive not only to tolerate but rather to foster initiative on the part of the personnel. It takes a very special kind of person to assume initiative under any circumstances because it often runs against a lifetime of conditioned fear responses. All of this conditioning is compounded in business and industry when personnel who have been put through "groveling training" are now asked to assume intrapreneurial initiative. In initiating, we use the same skills in relation to information as we use in relation to people in interpersonal processing.

"THROWING OUT A SKYHOOK"

Initiative is directionality emerging from the best available knowledge base. The key to initiative is that the initiator has conquered all available knowledge and skills in the area involved. Otherwise, initiative may be inappropriate. Put in other terms, before we can initiate productively, we must respond accurately to what is already there. Responding means that we have been inclusive of all available knowledge before initiating an exclusive direction. Thus, in addition to physical courage, initiative requires emotional empathy with the information environment surrounding us.

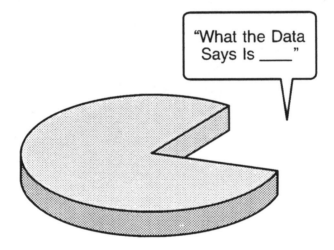

RESPONDING TO WHAT IS THERE

Based upon responding to what is there, we may respond additively to what is not there. Responding additively requires intimate knowledge of the data. It involves an intense experience with the data to extend the meaning and project the curves of the data. This level of emotional involvement implies a very special attitude of caring. The additive responder cares about the data as if they were people, for they do indeed represent the lives of people. Accordingly, the responder studies them so that in addition to noting what is present, he or she notes what is missing.

RESPONDING TO WHAT IS NOT THERE

146

Based upon this additive responsiveness to an inclusive knowledge base, initiative may be assumed. Initiative involves acting to fill a need or dealing in some way with what is not there in the picture we have developed. Thus, after developing an inclusive and additive base of experience, the initiator asserts an exclusive direction or goal. In so doing, the initiator defines the goal in terms of the operations needed to accomplish them and develops the systems to achieve the goals. In other words, the initiator is a processor, a manager of information who is directed by gaps in the information, or with a complete picture by the direction dictated by the information itself. Clearly, in addition to physical courage and emotional empathy, the initiator requires intellectual processing skills to transform the data of human experience into productive initiatives.

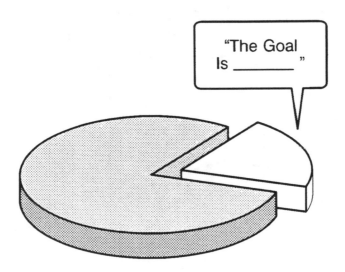

INITIATING TO FILL IN

Again, the key to initiative is the processing of an inclusive data base. It is this processing that yields a vision of the possible. The initiator first fills the gaps in information to paint a "perfect picture." In every situation, the initiator is developing a vision of the "ideal." It is in contrast with the "real" that the initiator finds the new direction. Thus, for example, in business, personnel may process information to create new and more productive systems for accomplishing goals. The executive can foster these visions by using interpersonal skills to communicate regularly with the personnel.

...A VISION OF PERFECTION...

While it is difficult to teach didactically, initiative may be modeled experientially. Indeed, the primary source of intra-preneurial initiative by organizational personnel is entrepreneurial initiative by executives. Entrepreneurial initiative is the initiative response produced by creative processing. Entrepreneurial initiative emphasizes creating new sources of variance at the policy-making level. This means processing the complex information in our environments and transforming it into manageable models and systems. Thus, complex information is factored and "captured" in delineated space and time to produce manageable models that empower organizations and personnel.

Entrepreneurial initiative by the executives may be imitated by the personnel in the organization. Where the entrepreneurs address sources of variance in the external environment, intrapreneurs tend to deal with internal sources of variance. However, both intrapreneurs and entrepreneurs process in the same manner. They respond accurately to develop an inclusive data base before initiating operationally to develop an exclusive direction. In responding, they must include external as well as internal sources of information. In initiating, they develop directions that are committed to the mission and, thus, the internal benefits of the organization. Empowering personnel to initiate intrapreneurially enables them to contribute to improving economic productivity growth.

INTRAPRENEURIAL POWER

It is important that the executive understand that what the initiator is really doing is creating variance. Variance is a technical term for the sources of effect or impact upon phenomena. People may understand the variance that has already been created with past discoveries. However, each new discovery creates new variance that dwarfs the significance of the previous amount of known variance. Thus, for example, in business, personnel may initiate to create new sources of variance in the systems: new resource inputs, new procedures or methods, new results outputs. The executive can foster these initiatives by creating a climate of experimentation and evaluation as the decision makers did with Sharon Fisher. Moreover, the real thrill and fulfillment for the executive is "throwing out a skyhook" to complete his or her own vision. Only the creative survive!

EXECUTIVE MEANING OF FREEING INITIATIVE

In summary, initiative is the single most difficult human dimension to develop:

> Initiative is creating new directions from the best available data bases by responding to what is missing.

It involves conquering all the skills involved in "working smarter." It is modeled after the initiative of others who are "potent reinforcers." It is committed to a mission outside oneself. In short, the mission and modeling mobilize individual resources to accomplish objectives leading toward the mission and beyond. All of these efforts and initiatives are evaluated and recycled as productivity feedback.

FREEING INITIATIVE ⟶ RECYCLING
PRODUCTIVITY FEEDBACK

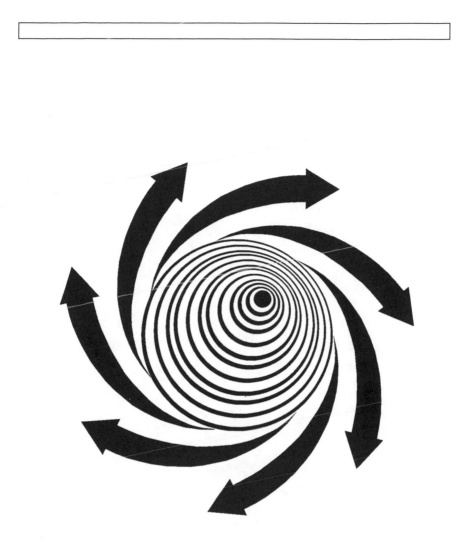

10. Recycle Feedback!

Ed Feder began the meeting by saying: "I know you're all wondering what a guy from personnel is doing in a place like this." Feder was a training manager of the Regional Exploration and Production Division of one of the major oil companies. The Division mission was to discover and develop oil fields. Here he was presenting to the executive vice president, a senior vice president, the regional vice president, and the executive committee of the Exploration Division. The topic was the purchase of new equipment. Feder was presenting on the Electronic Beam Recorder—what it is and does, and how it does it. With assistance, he was also presenting on the cost beneficial projections attached to using the new equipment. He had some anxiety regarding the meeting. The equipment was not in his special area of expertise. Human resource development was. He was also not an economist. Feder was fond of saying, "I can't even balance my checkbook." Yet here he was presenting cost-benefit projections. Feder also had confidence. The confidence came out of his track record with the company. His previous efforts had already produced millions of dollars in cost-avoidance and material, equipment, and job savings. His confidence came from the fact that he had the skills to "come out on the other side."

PROCESSING SKILLS

The corporate story began when Feder heard a small group of managers discussing their problems outside his office door. The problems revolved around "turnaround time" on the hard copies of seismic data. Committed to productivity improvement and being a problem-solver by nature and skill, Feder asked if he could "tag along" as the managers explored the problem. At Feder's behest, the managers brought all involved personnel together. He served as the group facilitator. He used his analytic skills to help the personnel define their problems. They had problems in planning and scheduling because they could not convert the miles of seismic data into "reprographic language." Several courses of action evolved out of a series of meetings. The managers "farmed out" the reprographics to local vendors. They determined to explore new technologies, including estimates of the costs and benefits of new photographic cameras. They even found valuable missing data that was stored in unmarked boxes.

The meetings had been an enormous success and Feder was the catalytic communicator that made it all possible. The interesting thing about the new equipment being considered was that it had already been rejected by the Research Department. Research was negative because its experts determined that in order to give back the seismic data needed, a very expensive, long-term effort of rewriting the software had to be undertaken. But Feder just kept on asking questions and getting more and more relevant information. He found that Research had studied the economics under inappropriate conditions. They did not understand that Exploration "worked off negatives" and, thus, Research employed the wrong criteria in making their recommendation. Instead, Feder found that the Electronic Beam Recorder promised to totally revolutionize how Exploration did things. The estimates were firm: with the new equipment Exploration could improve the quality of "reading" due to a better quality of negatives, thus, produce improved results outputs. In turn, reducing hard copy costs of seismic data would produce substantial cost savings. The hard copy savings would be in millions of dollars per year. The results benefits were inestimable, to be determined by future successes in discerning productive oil fields. Finally, the projections were that the equipment would be paid for in four to six months.

PROCESSING INFORMATION

The story of Ed Feder began a long time ago. Feder has a high energy level and good entrepreneurial instincts. He complemented his initiative skills with training in individual thinking, interpersonal processing skills, and organizational functions. Finally, he was specifically trained in solving problems through a team approach. There he learned to analyze and measure tasks in terms of quantity, quality, cost, and timeliness dimensions. He also learned to analyze performance problems in terms of their critical reasons: methods, machines, manpower and materials. But the real story of Feder is told in his love affair with information. He remains a humble and honest person. He does not consider himself a genius by any criteria. He simply employs his interpersonal processing and specialty skills to get enough information to solve problems and achieve goals in the most productive manner—most efficiently and effectively. Unlike most of the "experts" that we encounter on a daily basis, he does not use technical knowledge as a weapon, but rather as a lever that will multiply performance many times over. The real secret to his success is his joy in searching out, processing, and using information for productive purposes. He receives new information as it comes to him—innocent and virginal. he does not distort or abuse it for his private purposes. He simply helps it find its own conclusion. Feder experiences himself as merely accompanying the data in their drive to their own inevitable translation to usable information. Indeed, he becomes one with the latest integration of the data and, in so doing, culminates his own as well as the information's vitality. Feder had learned the secret of "making something out of nothing" through processing information.

MAKING SOMETHING OUT OF NOTHING

The results of Feder's productivity improvement programs may be viewed below. As can be seen, over a one-year period, in the seven projects that constituted the experiment, Feder and his associates were able to save more than $12 million through improving daily production and cost avoidance. In turn, the cost of the improvements in productivity were calculated at less than $1 million. Thus, the one-year return-on-investment was more than 12:1.

ORGANIZATIONAL PRODUCTIVITY OUTCOMES				
STUDY FOCUS	METHOD MEASURE	TIME	SAVINGS	COST
1. Reduce Flowline Back Pressure	Daily Production (Barrels of Oil)	1 Year	$ 1,440,000	$100,000
2. Increase Staff to Impact Lost Revenue	Daily Production	1 Year	$ 270,000	$100,000
3. Reduce Well Back Pressure	Daily Production	1 Year	$ 3,348,000	$537,500
4. Reduce Well Back Pressure	Daily Production	1 Year	$ 6,480,000	$150,000
5. Get Vessel to Work	Daily Production	1 Year	$ 182,500	$ 3,000
6. Eliminating Environmental Problems	Cost Avoidance	1 Year	$ 1,200	$ 730
7. Repairing Gas Plant	Daily Production	1 Year	$ 800,000	$100,000
		1 Year TOTALS	$12,521,700	$991,230

PRODUCTIVITY IMPROVEMENT

160

"Recycle feedback!" is the tenth strategy for economic growth. Productivity feedback involves a simple evaluation and comparison of results outputs and resource inputs. Obviously, in order to sustain an operation, the results outputs must exceed the resource inputs. With productive human processing, the resource inputs may be highly leveraged in relation to results outputs. Ultimately, the goal of human processing is to produce infinite results outputs. Ultimately, the goal of processing is to produce infinite results outputs while investing infinitesimal resource inputs.

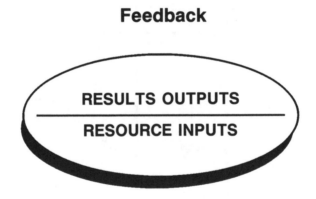

Feedback

RESULTS OUTPUTS
—————————————
RESOURCE INPUTS

PRODUCTIVITY FEEDBACK EMPHASIZES COMPARING RESULTS OUTPUTS WITH RESOURCE INPUTS

Another way of conceiving of productivity is in terms of effectiveness and efficiency. Effectiveness relates to results outputs. Efficiency relates to minimizing resource inputs. The substance of effectiveness always precedes the economies of efficiency.

Feedback

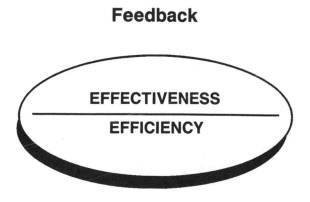

PRODUCTIVITY FEEDBACK EMPHASIZES COMPARING EFFECTIVENESS WITH EFFICIENCY

One major purpose of performance feedback is to facilitate self-supervision. Delivery personnel will use performance feedback to set and achieve higher standards than any supervisory monitoring could ever accomplish.

Performance Feedback

RESPONSE PERFORMANCE
RESOURCE INVESTMENT

PERFORMANCE FEEDBACK FACILITATES SELF-SUPERVISION

Remember the original mission? We targeted consumer populations. One of the purposes of feedback is to assess to what extent our products and services impacted or benefited the consumers. One way of assessing consumer benefits is to assess consumer productivity: Did our consumers become more effective in producing their results outputs while becoming more efficient in investing their resource inputs? Our business is to keep our consumers in business! We do this by helping them to become more productive through the use of our products and services.

Benefits Feedback

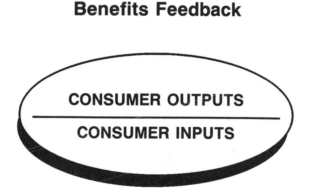

BENEFITS FEEDBACK FACILITATES
CONSUMER PRODUCTIVITY

Provided accelerated human processing of expanding information, productivity can be accelerated. It spirals to a point where we are producing literally infinite results outputs while simultaneously investing infinitesimal resource inputs, aside from the human and information resources which are processing this miracle. Human processing yields infinite human power.

Productivity Feedback

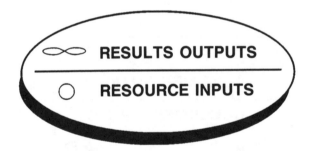

$$\frac{\infty \quad \text{RESULTS OUTPUTS}}{\bigcirc \quad \text{RESOURCE INPUTS}}$$

INFINITE HUMAN POWER

For the executive, the future belongs to an elite few who enjoy processing new information on a regular basis. These few enjoy the "press" of information just as good ball players responded to the challenge of a "full court press" in the Industrial Era. These people stand ready to dismantle established directions on a moment's notice with the introduction of new data just as modern ballplayers involved in a multiple-contingency offense. The problem is that the press of information accentuates the differences between performers. Whereas the differences in production of best to worst performers may have been one or two units per day during the Industrial Era, the differences in productivity between an exemplary performer and an ordinary performer in the Age of Information may now be 100 to 1 or even 1,000 to 1 or more. Because of an ability to use information, the exemplar is capable of producing significantly more results outputs with each production iteration. Moreover, the exemplars like Ed Feder produce these results while cutting resource investments with each iteration. For the executive, productivity is the exciting culmination of precious efforts and the promising projection of future efforts.

Executive Meaning of Productivity

To sum, all processing—organizational and individual—is recycled with productivity feedback:

Productivity feedback is simply the comparison of results outputs with resource inputs.

Productivity drives not merely on profitability. It drives upon our very humanity. For when we make the pie large enough for all to share, then shall we dare to become truly human. Only the productive grow!

RECYCLING PRODUCTIVITY FEEDBACK ⟶
IMPROVING PRODUCTIVITY

III. SUMMARY AND CONCLUSIONS—
THE INTERDEPENDENT LEADER AND POSITIONING FOR GROWTH

For the creative leader, it is already 1993! The only issue before him or her is this: how best to position my organization and its personnel for growth and viability. The basic components of the future corporations are human and information capital. The basic leadership functions are to empower organizations and personnel to unleash the awesome potential of these ingredients. The basic processes by which these empowering functions are accomplished emphasize the interdependent relationships of individual contributors—within and between people and organizations. It is 1993! Are you and your organization and its personnel positioned for growth and viability?

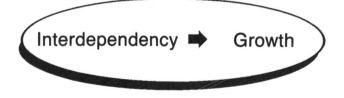

THE INTERDEPENDENT LEADER AND POSITIONING FOR GROWTH

The vehicle for empowering in the Age of the New Capitalism is interdependency. Indeed, empowering is inter-dependency. Interdependency is defined by the simultaneous and synergistic growth of people, organizations, and markets. The creative leader empowers people by enabling them to learn, perform, produce, and relate, both within the producer's organization in the workplace and between producer and consumer in the marketplace. In short, the creative leader in the Age of the New Capitalism is an interdependent leader. The interdependent leader empowers others so that he or she may be empowered by them.

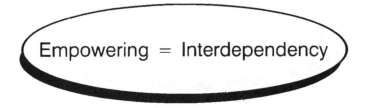

Empowering = Interdependency

THE INTERDEPENDENT LEADER

Historically, leadership was defined in terms of power. The leader ruled by controlling information. This was functional so long as that information was changing slowly. Today, the leader is besieged by information that is changing constantly and growing exponentially. Today and, perhaps forever, the creative leader will guide by empowering organizations and people to process the information. Indeed, leaders are empowered to the degree that they empower organizations and people to process information. Processing organizations and people return many times over the investment in skills and authority by their leaders. Each human brain possesses all of the intellectual power of the history of humankind, including our existing universe as we know it. By empowering people in human processing we begin to free this awesome brainpower. In turn, we are freed to employ our own brainpower. It is in the act of empowering that we are empowered.

EMPOWERING AND BEING EMPOWERED

We may summarize the principles of creative leadership. Again, these principles constitute a processing system for human productivity. As may be noted, the system is guided or driven by marketing information. The information is processed by a creative organization designed to maximize human processing. The productivity of the organization is actualized by personnel empowered to process and initiate. Productivity is evaluated and fed back to be processed as information input in the system. The system is a growing and spiraling system which frees both organizations and individuals to process and create productive information.

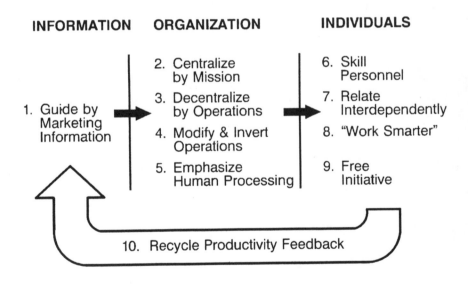

INFORMATION	ORGANIZATION	INDIVIDUALS
1. Guide by Marketing Information	2. Centralize by Mission 3. Decentralize by Operations 4. Modify & Invert Operations 5. Emphasize Human Processing	6. Skill Personnel 7. Relate Interdependently 8. "Work Smarter" 9. Free Initiative

10. Recycle Productivity Feedback

THE PRINCIPLES OF CREATIVE LEADERSHIP

In this context, you may review and plot the ratings of your own levels of leadership. Simply rate yourself in terms of tendency and time in relation to the following questions.

1. Are you guided by marketing information?
2. Is your organization centralized by a well-defined mission?
3. Is your organization decentralized by operations?
4. Is your organization modified to maximize information processing?
5. Does your organization emphasize human processing?
6. Are your personnel skilled in thinking?
7. Do your personnel relate interdependently?
8. Do your personnel "work smarter"?
9. Do you free your personnel to initiate?
10. Do you recycle productivity information feedback?

Executive
Levels of Functioning

Creative
Principles

	Low		Minimum		High
	1	2	3	4	5
	None of Time	Some of Time	Minimal Time	Most of Time	All of Time
1. Marketing Information					
2. Centralized Operations					
3. Decentralized Operations					
4. Modified Operations					
5. Human Processing					
6. Skilled Personnel					
7. Interdependent Relations					
8. "Smart Workers"					
9. Freed Initiative					
10. Recycle Productivity					

DIAGNOSING EXECUTIVE LEVELS OF FUNCTIONING

At the same time that you rate where you are currently functioning, you may also rate where you would like to function. Furthermore, if you rate yourself above level 3 on any principle, you may want to invest in longer-term development programs to improve your functioning as well as that of your organization and personnel. If you rate below level 3 on any dimension, you need to invest in immediate action programs.

	Executive			
Creative	**Levels of Functioning**			
Principles	Low	Minimum		High
	1	2	3	4	5
1. Marketing				
2. Centralized				
3. Decentralized				
4. Modified				
5. Processing				
6. Skilled				
7. Interdependent				
8. Smart				
9. Initiative				
10. Productivity				

TRIGGERING ACTION PROGRAMS

The implications for executives are profound. We stand at a window of opportunity. Approximately 85 percent of growth in economic productivity is accounted for by human and information capital development. Those creative leaders who empower their organizations in information processing and empower their personnel in human processing skills will reap a harvest of extraordinary productivity and growth. Those executives who do not will not be around in executive roles—either in 1993 or at any time—for their organizations will no longer exist in the way that they now know them!

BIBLIOGRAPHY

Baldwin, W. "Creative Destruction." *Forbes*, July 13, 1987.

Bennett, A. "Growing Small." *Wall Street Journal*, May 4, 1987.

Berenson, B.G. "The Business of Business is Education." *Personal Communication*. April, 1987.

Birch, D.L. "The Atomization of America." *INC.*, March, 1987.

Blundell, W.E. "Failure: Spotlight on a Neglected Side of Business." *Wall Street Journal*, December 15, 1986, p. 29.

Boyer, C. "In Orlando, It Was the Customers Who Came Calling." *Think*, 1987, 53, 2-5.

Browne, M.W. "Physicist Aims to Create a Universe, Literally." *New York Times*, April 14, 1987.

Carkhuff, R.R. *Sources of Human Productivity*. Amherst, Mass.: Human Resource Development Press, 1983.

Carkhuff, R.R. *The Exemplar—The Exemplary Performer in the Age of Productivity*. Amherst, Mass.: Human Resource Development Press, 1985.

Carkhuff, R.R. *The Age of the New Capitalism*. Amherst, Mass.: Human Resource Development Press, 1988.

Carkhuff, R.R. *Human Processing and Human Productivity*. Amherst, Mass.: Human Resource Development Press, 1986.

Carkhuff, R.R. and Cannon, J.R. *The Exemplary Organization in the Age of Information*. McLean, VA: Carkhuff Institute of Human Technology, 1986.

Carnavale, A.P. *Human Capital*. Washington, D.C.: American Society for Training and Development, 1983.

Clements, J. "The Turbulent Job Market." *Forbes*, July 13, 1987.

Cleveland, H. "Information as a Resource." In E. Cornish, Editor, *Careers Tomorrow*. Bethesda, MD: World Future Society, 1983.

Finegan, J. "Four-Star Management." *INC.*, January 1987.

Gilbert, T.F. *Human Competence*. New York: McGraw-Hill, 1978.

Grayson, C.J. *The U.S. Economy and Productivity.* Washington, D.C.: Joint Economics Committee, 1980.

Hartman, C. "Who's Running American's Fastest Growing Companies?" *INC.*, August 1983.

Hartman, C. "Inside the *INC.* 500." *INC.*, December 1984.

Kahn, J.P. "Raising the Roof." *INC.*, December 1986.

Kaplan, G.M. "Boosting Word Processing Productivity by 80%." *LIST*, December 1983.

Kichen, S., Popp, D. and Wagstaff, M. "The Boss." *Forbes*, 1987, 139, June 15, 1987.

London, H.I. "Death of the University." *The Futurist*, 21, 17–22.

Macdonald, C.R. *Performance Based Supervisory Development.* Amherst, Mass.: Human Resource Development Press, 1982.

Malabra, A.L. *Beyond Our Means.* New York: Random House, 1987.

Miller, M.M. and Gray, P.B. "Why Businesses Often Sink in 'Decisional Quicksand.'" *Wall Street Journal*, December 15, 1986, p. 29.

Nayak, P.R. and Kettringham, J.M. "The Fine Art of Managing Creativity." *New York Times*, November 2, 1986, p. F2.

Newcomb, P. "No One Is Safe." *Forbes*, July 13, 1987.

Prokesch, S. "The Remaking of the American C.E.O." *New York Times*, January 25, 1987.

Reich, R.B. "Enterprise and Double Cross." *Washington Monthly,* January 1987.

Rhodes, L. and Amend, P. "The Turnaround." *INC.*, August 1986.

Roper Organization, *The Public Pulse*, 1986, Vol. 1, Number 11.

Sanoff, A.P. "Risk Takers." *U.S. News and World Report,* January 26, 1987.

Shilling, G. "Face-to-Face." *INC.*, November 1986.

Simpson, J.C. "Business Schools—and Students—Want to Talk Only About Success." *Wall Street Journal*, December 15, 1986, p. 29.

Smith, F. "Face-to-Face." *INC.*, October 1986.

Tichy, N.M. and Devanna, M.A. "The Transformational Leader." *Training and Development Journal*, 1986, Volume 40, 27–32.

Waldman, P. "Motivate or Alienate? Firms Hire Gurus to Change Their Culture." *Wall Street Journal*, July 24, 1987.

Wessel, D. "First, Ask the Right Questions." *Wall Street Journal*, June 12, 1987.

Wishard, W.V.D. "The 21st Century Economy." *The Futurist*, 21, 23–38.

Zemke, R. "The Honeywell Studies—How Managers Learn to Manage." *Training*, 1985, Volume 22, 46–51.